EARLY PRAISE FOR WHEN WOMEN TALK: DEFYING SOCIAL EXPECTATIONS

"Every story in *When Women Talk* volume 2 is a powerful reminder that our circumstances do not define us—our choices do. With honesty and courage, these women shatter norms, transforming hardship into triumph and inspiring us to embrace our true selves and forge our own paths. This collection is a rallying cry for those ready to redefine limits and step into power."
—Paula Skaper, founder, 33Dolphins Growth Strategy

"*When Women Talk* is an inspiring and deeply moving collection of stories that reveal the strength, resilience, and courage of women who have defied expectations. These powerful narratives will have you laughing, crying, and cheering as each woman shares her journey of overcoming obstacles and creating a life on her own terms. This book is a must-read for anyone seeking motivation and proof that no matter our circumstances, we can choose to rise, redefine success, and step into our full potential."
—Kanwal Trehan, CEO & founder, SheBIZ

"Courageous women in this book shatter limits, choosing to turn challenges into triumphs. Their inspiring stories—spanning cultural, personal, and professional battles—urge us to rethink our potential and ignite change. Each heartfelt and authentic story invites you to redefine your limits, reclaim your power, and ignite a transformational shift in your mindset and life."
—Sandy Gerber, Certified Communication & Emotional Intelligence Coach, speaker & author, *Emotional Magnetism: How to Communicate to Ignite Connection in Your Relationships*

"These deeply personal stories are encouraging, inspiring, and truly uplifting. Each contributing author brings a unique and deeply personal perspective, sharing moments of hardship, perseverance, and ultimately, triumph. Their willingness to be vulnerable and honest makes this book not just inspiring, but also deeply relatable. It's a celebration of unlikely heroes who fought hard so they could be the narrator of their own story. These women have defied social expectations, broken through barriers, and emerged stronger, proving that empowerment comes from within.

"*When Women Talk* is a lived experience. Whether you're facing challenges yourself or seeking motivation to take charge of your life, this book will leave you feeling ready to embrace your own power. I highly recommend it to anyone looking for a dose of inspiration and a reminder that no matter the circumstances, there is always a way forward."

—Sam Chung, CEO & founder, Elletourage

VOLUME 2

WHEN WOMEN TALK

VOLUME 2

DEFYING SOCIAL EXPECTATIONS

CURATED BY **CATHY KUZEL**

Published by

North Vancouver, British Columbia, Canada
WhenWomenTalk.ca

Cover and text design by Carly Franklin, BOOST Design + Marketing
Copy-editing and proofreading by Naomi Pauls, Paper Trail Publishing

Publisher's Cataloguing-in-Publication data

Kuzel, Cathy, editor.
When women talk , volume 2 : defying social expectations / curated by Cathy Kuzel.
North Vancouver, BC: The Connected Woman, 2025.
ISBN: ISBN 978-1-7380791-1-7 (paperback) | 978-1-7380791-2-4 (e-book)
LCSH Women—Biography. | Women executives—Biography. | Businesswomen—Canada—Biography. | Entrepreneurship. | Leadership in women. | Success in business. | BISAC BIOGRAPHY & AUTOBIOGRAPHY / Women | BIOGRAPHY & AUTOBIOGRAPHY / Business | BUSINESS & ECONOMICS / Entrepreneurship | BUSINESS & ECONOMICS / Motivational
LCC HD6054.3 .W44 2025 | DDC 658.4/092—dc23

To the women who focus on the value of their voice and do not seek approval to use it.

CONTENTS

Dear Reader / 1

Choose Your Own Path *by Kimberly McLaren* / 5

Ninety-seven Cents and a Dream *by Michelle Bond* / 17

A Journey to Joy *by Flora Joy Lakey* / 31

From My First Breath *by Marilyn R. Wilson* / 45

Your Story Is Your Choice *by Samantha Day* / 59

Honouring Our True Selves *by Rino Murata* / 73

Letting Go with Grace *by Jaz Gill* / 87

The Courage to Change *by Shannon Little* / 101

Give Yourself Permission *by Gina Best* / 115

There Is No Alternative *by Fiona Forestell* / 129

About Cathy Kuzel / 143

Due to the personal nature of these stories, the content includes details that could be distressing to some readers.

DEAR READER

In 2023 the first volume of *When Women Talk* was curated and released. The anthology's publication marked the fifteenth anniversary of the women's community I had created—The Connected Woman® Association in Vancouver, British Columbia, Canada. That book project was meant to be a "one and done," however, it was so well received that I began to get inquiries as to when the second volume would be published. Eighteen months and 67 author submissions later, volume 2 is a reality.

When Women Talk volume 2 is a collection of life stories from ten remarkable women, whose stories were chosen to ignite innovation, create a willingness to embrace self-belief, and to help us understand that we can adapt to changing circumstances and seize opportunities by defying societal expectations based on who we are, where we are from, where we live, our background, or circumstances over which we had no control.

Societal expectations. Social norms. We've all grown up with them. We might not think we have, but consider the traditions that we usually adhere to "just because." How many times have we done or become something because it was expected of us? Although many of these norms have a purpose, some limit us from being who we truly are, from reaching our inherent potential.

These expectations become self-limiting beliefs, and then we set boundaries based on these beliefs, these fears, these perceived limitations, which prevent us from becoming our best selves. Social expectations can dictate what we should or shouldn't do by shaping our choices and influencing what we believe in—what we believe is achievable. They become a self-fulfilling prophesy.

Defying expectations takes a lot of strength and determination because it challenges the status quo. Within these pages, the authors share some very intense stories about how they defied social expectations placed on them, how they have challenged societal norms to create a life for themselves, for their family, a life that resonates with them. Each chapter offers a unique insight into the effect social norms can have on our mental and physical well-being and how they can hold us "prisoner" by our own thoughts. By choosing to change a subconscious mindset to a more intentional one, these women have changed their circumstances, creating a new direction, a new outcome.

Some of the stories shared in this book are not for the faint of heart, since they contain details and experiences that none of us want to experience first-hand. But they are told with the hope that these stories and experiences will challenge our perception of what is possible and encourage us to pursue our dreams. Perhaps these stories may even create a shift to challenge biases and stereotypes that exist in our society.

By defying expectations together, we can create a place where individual potential knows no bounds, where we are celebrated for who we are and, first and foremost, we have a strong belief in ourselves.

Cathy

For me, words are a form of action, capable of influencing change. Their articulation represents a complete, lived experience.—Ingrid Bengis

CHOOSE YOUR OWN PATH
BY KIMBERLY McLAREN

For some people, being employed by someone else may be exactly what they need, and it may provide just the right fit for their lifestyle. For me, and for most entrepreneurial people, it just wasn't enough.

THE YEAR WAS 1966, and I was born in the middle of a decade that saw the seeds of change planted for women. Change is still growing from those seeds, but we have not transformed society yet. There is still work to be done. We know what we want, but society is not fully on board.

The year was 1984, and I did what society expected of me: I graduated from high school and started making plans to further my education. Not knowing exactly what I wanted to do, I took general college courses until deciding to enrol in a business management program and graduated with a diploma in 1989. My life was falling in line with generally accepted regularity. I knew my career path was destined to be in the financial field, so I enrolled in the CGA program and embarked on the long road to becoming a Certified General Accountant.

The year was 1993. I had met a man, fallen in love, and that year I got married. I had dreams of living my life beside this man and raising our children together. He had a great job, so we decided that I would stay at home with the kids and work part time as I continued my studies in the CGA program. With my husband's steady income, I would be able to start a little accounting practice after I graduated, with no pressure. It was a lovely dream—until everything came crashing down around me.

Our first child was born in 1995, followed by the second in 1998. That same year, my husband and I bought our first home, in the Fraser Valley. I had lived my whole life in North Vancouver, so this was a big move for me. We were so happy, for a while. But the pressures of parenthood, home ownership, and life in general took their toll, and in the year 2001, my world collapsed. My husband was gone. I was a single mother, working part time and raising two young children. I was lost. I didn't know what I was going to do. Child support never came and in short order, my now ex-husband disappeared. I was alone with broken dreams, but I had to figure out something for those two young children depending on me. So I focused on survival, found more work, finished the CGA program, and graduated in 2006. I had found full-time work by then, but when I graduated, I started the little accounting practice I had once dreamed of having. At least I could salvage some of my original dreams!

Stepping up to full-time self-employment

Things were good for a few years. The kids and I were happy, my career was stable, and even though things had not turned out as I had expected, I was creating a good life for us. However, by 2009, another blow came when I lost my full-time job. Facing reduced income, I did what I thought made the most sense. I decided to expand my part-time accounting practice and began to search for new clients. I already had a part-time practice, so it seemed logical to just take that to a new level and run the business full time. At least the plan made sense to me. I quickly realized that society had different expectations for me in my current situation.

When I proudly announced that I was taking my practice to

full-time status, I was met by disbelief and shock. People close to me told me I couldn't do that because I needed to have a real job, since I was a single mom with responsibilities. I was told

> *I started to doubt myself and wonder if I had made the wrong decision. Could I do this on my own? Could I put the time into my business and still have time for my responsibilities as a mom?*

that I would never be successful on my own. How could I run a business on my own *and* look after my family? I was told to go find a job working for an already established firm. But I'd already done that, and it did not provide what I needed financially, nor did it provide an environment where I could thrive personally. To me it was clear that I needed to push forward with my own practice. But the pushback I received was real and kept coming. I started to doubt myself and wonder if I had made the wrong decision. Could I do this on my own? Could I put the time into my business and still have time for my responsibilities as a mom? I spent many sleepless nights. Finding clients was taking longer than I had hoped, so that doubt just kept creeping in. I almost gave in to the pressure to find more acceptable employment, but my stubbornness kept driving me forward.

It wasn't easy but I did eventually find my first new client. That client, along with many others, is still with me today.

Landing that client propelled me to continue moving forward with my plans, despite being constantly told that I was making a mistake. One by one I added new clients, and slowly the practice grew to a full-time status. Running a business, any business, is not easy. Ensuring you have a steady stream of income can be a challenge. And as a single mother, a single parent for that matter, steady income is even more important apparently. But who says that it is? Who says that you can't be ahead of the game or find ways to survive when there are delays in your income stream?

Eventually I did what I set out to do and built a practice that provided full-time income. Self-employment comes with its pros

> *Do single mothers look a certain way? Do we have features that distinguish us from married mothers? I don't believe that is the case, nor do I believe that society can dictate what our careers look like.*

and cons, and one of the biggest advantages as a single parent was that working for myself afforded me more time with my children. I was able to adjust my work schedule and be present in their lives. Attending school functions, events, and concerts during school hours became something I was able to do, while many of the employed parents had to miss out. I was able to take my children on a five-week trip to Europe and teach them so many incredible things about travel and other countries, people, and traditions. Many of the employed parents of my children's friends were not able to do the things I was able to do because their available holiday time was restricted. And yet, still I felt the pressure to conform and find employment rather than to continue operating my practice.

There was a stereotype of what a single mom looked like. Once, at a soccer game while watching one of my children play, I overheard other parents chatting about a single mom at their school. I was asked for my opinion, and I replied that perhaps I was not the best person to ask, considering I was a single mom. These parents were shocked and said that they had no idea. Do single mothers look a certain way? Do we have features that distinguish us from married mothers? I don't believe that is the case, nor do I believe that society can dictate what our careers look like. If I had conformed to social expectations or given in to the pressures, I don't believe the life I was building for my kids would have been better. Being an employee would have limited my ability to be present. I finally knew I had made the right decision. But my story did not end there.

Facing pushback and negativity a second time

In 2016 I became very sick and had to take an extended period of time off work. Luckily, I had been able to set aside some savings, which allowed me to take the required time off. But due to not being able to keep up with the workload, I had to let some clients go. This meant rebuilding my practice once I was able. It felt like I was back to square one, but surely the pressures I had felt the first time would not impact establishing my business this time. I was wrong.

Apparently, now I was not only a single mom but also too old to be working for myself, and I needed the stability that an employment situation would provide. Having built up my business previously and experienced the pushback before, I knew that if I persevered, I would succeed. I was saddened that society had not progressed and that I was still impacted by the idea that single moms should not be self-employed. "It's simply too risky," people said. Now I faced the added misconception that I was too old to rebuild, and I should just work for someone else. I should hold steady, comfortable, regular jobs and not take any risks. "Don't push yourself to do more," is what I heard. "Just accept the status quo so that we in society can be comfortable with our decisions." I refused to accept this mindset and kept pushing myself. I knew that the life my kids and I had was not always easy because I was self-employed, but it was also full of experiences and memories that neither they nor I will ever forget—because I was self-employed.

What have I learned from all this? I learned that my children loved the times that I was able to spend with them as much as I enjoyed those times. Could I have spent that time with them if I was someone else's employee? Yes, I probably could still have spent some time with them, but maybe not when it counted most. But control over my schedule was not the only thing self-employment gave me. Having my own business did other things for me personally. It gave me direction and a sense of accomplishment that I had not felt as an employee. It allowed me to work in an environment where I thrived. For some people, being employed by someone else may be exactly what they need, and it may provide just the right fit for their lifestyle. For me, and for most entrepreneurial people, it just wasn't enough.

Whether you choose to be an employee or to be self-employed, always choose your own path, and don't allow others or society in general to dictate what that path looks like. Making your own way may not always be easy, but never be afraid to defy social expectations. Live the life you want, not one defined by others.

KIMBERLY McLAREN

Kimberly resides in the beautiful Fraser Valley of British Columbia. She has two adult children and lives with her best friend and sidekick—a malamute husky cross named Skye. She has a connection with and deep love for all animals and nature, and life would not be the same without a dog by her side. Kimberly loves to travel and learn, read a good book by a cozy fireplace, and spend time reflecting on how grateful she is to be alive.

Kimberly's mission as a Chartered Professional Accountant is to help businesses, large and small, and any individual when it comes to taxes, bookkeeping, and all things numbers related. As an entrepreneur who started her business from the ground up not once but twice, she knows the importance of having knowledgeable, reliable people involved in your business.

Kimberly also loves providing assistance to youth, teaching them tax basics, how to budget, and other information regarding personal or business finances.

- ⊕ cpakm.ca
- ⊙ cpakm
- f cpakmltd

NINETY-SEVEN CENTS AND A DREAM

BY MICHELLE BOND

People like to say, "Real estate is always risky." Sure. But if you crunch the numbers and track the local market, a so-called risk might be an opportunity in disguise.

I WAS TWENTYSOMETHING, broke, and living in a dingy three-bedroom apartment with two revolving roommates, one of whom was my former classmate. It was 2005, and I was teetering on the edge of burnout. My entire life felt like a precarious balancing act—working at a new position in film as a production assistant, waitressing or banquet serving for barely any money, and constantly trying to figure out if I could return to finish my teaching degree. Just a couple of years earlier, I'd started my bachelor of education, but after witnessing a tragic accident where I was working as a waitress, it derailed me so completely that I missed classes and was forced to withdraw. I sank into depression, lost financial aid, and came close to bankruptcy.

On top of that, I was juggling a line of credit and credit card loaded with about twenty grand in debt, plus student loans totalling approximately $24,000. I was running on fumes. Most of my paycheques went straight to covering overdue bills and rent. Forget a savings account—day-to-day life was a scramble.

Home at the time was in an area jokingly called "Burquitlam," right on the border between Burnaby and Coquitlam. Picture an apartment shared by three broke students, each paying rent in the $240 to $290 range. Back then, even $700 or $800 per month felt like a fortune. I couldn't handle that on my own, which is why I ended up in the three-bedroom.

Our landlord could charitably be described as "unpredictable." He was often high and would show up at midnight, ranting about random grievances. One time he banged on my door at 1:00 a.m. to complain about a truck he claimed was in the wrong parking spot—despite the fact that nobody in our place even had a truck. I was beyond ready to get out of there.

> *If this student featured in the newspaper could do it, why couldn't I? Sure, I had no real down payment and was drowning in debt, but I also had the clarity to know that the biggest obstacle was just getting started.*

I'd earned my bachelor of arts degree in 2003 from Simon Fraser University (SFU), but my plan to go straight into education had been sidelined. Now, instead of having a stable teacher's salary, I was scrambling for income. I snagged my first job as a production assistant in film around June 2005. I liked film work well enough—there was a sense of camaraderie on set, and the pay was decent if you could keep landing gigs. But even with that, I was still living close to the edge. Honestly, the only reason I didn't end up out on the street was a random batch of credit-card "convenience cheques" that the bank mailed me one day just when I was tapped out on my line of credit. I used them to pay my rent until the cheques were fully maxed out too— my Hail Mary pass before the film gig materialized. By then I had zero dollars to my name and zero credit available. That first paycheque from the film job arrived just in time to save me from eviction and starvation.

The undying real estate dream

Despite all this chaos, one dream continued to smoulder in the back of my mind: *I want to buy my own home.* Since I was fourteen, I had told anyone who'd listen that I didn't ever want to pay someone else's mortgage and would stop doing so the minute I could. I had always been brushed aside as a daydreamer. Pretty much every time I expressed any big ambition—"I want to own a home," "I want to get my teaching credentials," "I want to work in film"—my family dismissed me.

After a brief cost-saving stint at Douglas College for my first and second years, I had started at SFU in 2000 and graduated with my BA in visual art and theatre production in 2003. Sometime in those undergrad years, I picked up a free student newspaper on campus and read a story that changed my life. It detailed how a fellow student had bought multiple pre-sale condos in the Lower Mainland and flipped his way into a million-dollar penthouse. He had started modestly—small deposits on pre-build properties that rose in value by the time they were completed, allowing him to refinance or sell and take the profit. Then he'd repeat the cycle. His was not an overnight rags-to-riches tale; it was more like a methodical, step-by-step process—something that seemed possible for an ordinary person. And best of all, you only needed 5 percent down on a pre-sale condo back in the early to mid 2000s.

I couldn't stop thinking about that story, as I watched Vancouver's market explode in real time. Whenever a new building went up in Burquitlam or Coquitlam, by the time it was complete, the units had jumped in value by tens of thousands of dollars. If this student featured in the newspaper could do it, why couldn't I? Sure, I had no real down payment and was drowning in debt, but I also had the clarity to know that the biggest obstacle was just getting started.

That summer of 2005, a postcard was slipped under my apartment door advertising a new pre-sale development down the street, right next to Lougheed Mall and a major transit hub. It was the ideal location for commuting to SFU, Vancouver, or just about anywhere. One glance at the postcard and my heart rate skyrocketed: *this was it.*

I couldn't afford it, of course. But that had never stopped me from dreaming or scheming. Checking out the display suite couldn't hurt. So one day, wearing my usual student attire— scruffy jogging pants, an old SFU T-shirt, and my white pom-pom toque that my cousin said made me look like a Q-tip—I walked in. I was going to buy one of these places.

Down payment on a one-bedroom

The showroom was busy—young professionals, older couples, and a few foreign investors snapping up multiple units. I stood out like a sore thumb. When a salesperson approached me, I told her I was interested in a one-bedroom. She showed me a gorgeous floor plan: an L-shaped, open-concept suite with modern design and amazing building amenities—an outdoor pool, hot tub, yoga studio, indoor minigolf, fitness centre, and clubhouse lounge with a kitchen. I could picture myself actually living there. I was 100 percent sold.

"Are you ready to secure one today?" she asked.

"I . . . I'd like to," I stammered. "But I don't have the down payment yet."

"That's okay," she said. "We don't need the full down payment until closing. Just some kind of collateral to hold a unit."

I laughed nervously. In my pocket, all I had was loose change—literally ninety-seven cents. It was so absurd I almost felt compelled to show her the coins as a joke. "I only have this," I told her, dropping the handful of change onto the counter.

To my astonishment, she barely flinched. "If that's what you have, we can take it," she said, with a polite, encouraging smile.

You'd think I would have felt relieved, but it was more like shock. Was this really happening? Did I just—unintentionally— hand over ninety-seven cents as a deposit on a piece of real estate? The salesperson even snapped a photo of the coins to attach to my file. Then she slid the paperwork in front of me. We signed forms, she mentioned a promotional rate from a local bank, and I walked out in a daze. I now "owned" a pre-sale condo on paper but in reality, I needed $13,000 for the 5 percent down payment before closing. I wasn't sure how I'd get it.

I knew the only chance was to ask my parents. If anyone could give or lend me $13,000, it was them. I also knew my dad might be skeptical if I asked but I had a plan: I'd been reading about how, once the condo was built, I could refinance up to 80 percent of its newly appraised value, pay back my parents in full, and keep any extra equity as cash. *Everybody wins*, I thought.

When I sat down with them, I came armed with data. I showed them how pre-sale units in that neighbourhood were consistently selling for much more by the time buildings were complete. I had the article from the student newspaper. I had real estate comps. I had a timeline for paying them back. They stared at me like I'd just told them I was moving to Mars—but, miraculously, my dad finally sighed and said, "Fine. I'll lend you the money. But I want it back as soon as you can refinance."

This was me claiming my future. And so, with my dad's reluctant approval, I had the $13,000 lined up.

> *During those months, I felt every shade of anxiety. What if the market tanked? What if the bank didn't approve me with a co-signer? What if something went wrong with the construction?*

Completion, refinancing, and repeat

Pre-sales in real estate often take anywhere from eighteen months to two years to complete. For me, that was time to (1) pray the market remained strong, and (2) start building a stable credit profile so I could qualify for the mortgage. By late 2005, I was working in film regularly, paying down some of my debts, and trying to keep a lid on expenses. My plan was simple: Survive until the building is done. Then refinance, pay Dad back, and possibly walk away with extra equity.

During those months, I felt every shade of anxiety. What if the market tanked? What if the bank didn't approve me with a co-signer? What if something went wrong with the construction?

Less than two years after I put down those ninety-seven cents, the building was completed. The day I stepped into my new unit, the hallways smelled of fresh paint, the elevator was protected with plastic for the moving crews, and the floors were so new they gleamed. It felt surreal. I'd gone from having a nightmarish Burquitlam crackhead landlord to owning a condo in a top-notch building. When I finalized my mortgage, the appraised value of my unit came back at around $331,000—a staggering jump from my original purchase price of $215,000. Suddenly I had over $115,000 in equity just by virtue of buying early.

I wasted no time marching into the bank after I took possession. Yes, I was petrified. But I'd done my homework: I would refinance up to 80 percent of the new appraised value and have roughly $49,000 of accessible equity after paying out the mortgage plus fees. Out of that, I paid back my dad his $13,000. I still had about $36,000 left to invest again and pay off some debts.

The look on the bank clerk's face was one of pure annoyance. They figured I'd be locked into the original mortgage rate forever. But I was a newly minted real estate investor, and I was calling the shots. *In my twenties.* Broke and depressed only a couple of years earlier, now I had $35,000 in my bank account, with a fully owned (well, mortgaged) condo. I was over the moon.

With my leftover equity, I did exactly what the student in the newspaper had done: I put a deposit on another pre-sale, this one up on Burnaby Mountain near SFU, right above Nesters Market—a spot that was rapidly developing with cafés, restaurants, and new shops. I also tackled some of my student loan debt. This was how you climbed the real estate ladder in Vancouver. It wasn't magic, and it wasn't easy. It took planning, numbers, and nerves of steel. But it worked.

One of the biggest takeaways was realizing that I didn't need anybody's faith in me—just a feasible plan. My family's skepticism fuelled a certain self-determination in me, and ironically, that self-determination became a superpower. Every time they refused to acknowledge my achievements, I just worked harder. I wanted to prove my worth. But more than that, I wanted to prove to myself that I could shape my own destiny, no matter how broke or in debt I was.

Lessons in risk, reward, and resourcefulness

If there's one moment that encapsulates the gamble of real estate investment I made, it's plunking ninety-seven cents on that sales desk. It was an action at once ridiculous, terrifying, and empowering. It epitomized the fact that sometimes all you have is pocket change and sheer determination. The real estate market was a wild ride, but I'd studied it for years, read that article in the SFU newspaper, and saw how pre-sale properties in prime locations almost always rose in value. Armed with that knowledge, I forged ahead.

The experience taught me a crucial lesson about risk-taking: there's a big difference between blind risk and educated risk. People like to say, "Real estate is always risky." Sure. But if you crunch the numbers and track the local market, a so-called risk might be an opportunity in disguise. I had no blueprint to follow other than that old newspaper article, but it was enough to get me started. In business or in personal finance, research plus bravery tends to go a long way.

I also learned about resourcefulness. When you don't have a nest egg of your own, you might have to find it elsewhere—co-signers, creative financing, line-of-credit cheques, or day-and-night hustle. Nobody was going to hand me a golden ladder, so I grabbed onto my family's reluctant generosity and used it like a rung, climbing up to the next rung and the next. Without personal connections or a big support system, all I had was my willpower, my knowledge, and my ability to make a compelling case for a family loan.

Finally, through investing in real estate, I discovered a new level of self-confidence. For the first time in my life, I'd done something that utterly shocked even me. I'd been depressed, broke, yet I owned a condo in a sought-after area before turning thirty. I wasn't a burden; I was building a future. And I knew the truth: I was the only person I needed to believe in me.

That first purchase was the catalyst. It reshaped my trajectory in real estate and beyond. Once you see that it's possible to turn almost nothing into tens of thousands of dollars in equity, you start to see doors where everyone else sees walls. After the pre-sale on Burnaby Mountain, I started looking at other creative ways to invest, at times teaming up with partners or using various financial strategies I'd researched. Not every endeavour went as smoothly as buying that first condo, but each one taught me a new skill. And with every success, I realized I'd broken free from the idea that I needed someone else's approval to thrive, and by defying social expectations, I was succeeding.

In a city like Vancouver, the odds are rarely in your favour if you're young, broke, and carrying loads of student debt. But sometimes the biggest leaps come from the darkest corners of desperation. That's what 2005 felt like for me: a wobbly combination of desperation, determination, and the glimmer of a half-remembered newspaper article. The day I walked out of that sales centre with the Polaroid picture of my ninety-seven-cent deposit, I'd never felt more alive or more petrified. And that feeling—fear braided with elation—turned out to be the most potent motivator of all.

Would I recommend that everyone leverage themselves to the hilt if they're buried in student debt? Not necessarily. My success resulted from a combination of market timing, location research, and my willingness to fight for a future I believed in. But I do encourage people to trust their instincts, put in the legwork, and ask for help—even if it means risking a no. You might be surprised, as I was, to find that all it takes is ninety-seven cents to hold your place in line for the life you want.

MICHELLE BOND

With a background in theatre, hotel sales, and arts education, Michelle earned multiple credentials, including a bachelor of education, a bachelor of arts, and a certificate in criminology. During her twenties, in the face of immense personal challenges, she pursued her dream of home ownership by putting a tiny down payment on a pre-sale condo without knowing where the balance would come from. Her story of how she started investing in real estate is a testament to perseverance, creativity, and self-belief.

Michelle's career spans the film industry, where she works as an assistant director, location scout, and set dresser. In addition, she is the co-author of the *Production Assistant Survival Guide* for the Directors Guild of Canada, BC.

She is now a BC-certified teacher in West Vancouver, regularly volunteering in her community and investing in boutique hotels.

A passionate adventurer, Michelle values family, perseverance, and collaboration, and continues to inspire others with her unwavering determination.

- 🌐 exploredreamscapes.com
- 🌐 propertiesbymichelle.ca
- in linkedin.com/in/michelle-bond-b-a-bed-1811ab183/

A JOURNEY TO JOY
BY FLORA JOY LAKEY

As I do my decolonizing work in the school system, I am decolonizing myself. And this will be a lifelong journey.

Dedicated to all the ancestors who hid in secret to practise our songs, language, dances, and ceremonies at the risk of jail, so that these practices still remain and can be taught to the next generation.

HOW ON SACRED MOTHER EARTH did I ever end up working in a school? I don't even like kids. They can be so annoying! But isn't that the magic of life, when you end up somewhere completely unexpected only to discover your purpose in the last place you would ever look?

As an Indigenous child, I, along with two of my siblings, was thrust into a white, Christian upper-middle-class environment as part of the Sixties Scoop in British Columbia. I was four and a half. Growing up, school was a torture chamber of violence and racism, which taught me strong survival skills and little else. In Grade 9 we were studying Canadian history and I noticed that every time the soldiers attacked an Indigenous community, it was a battle and there were heroes, yet every time the Indigenous warriors attacked a fort or settlement, they were bloodthirsty heathens. *Oh my God, I am a heathen and all that goes with it*, and in that moment that became my self-image. I never told anyone I was Indigenous for the next thirty years. By the time I graduated from high school and left my adopted home at eighteen, the concept was firmly planted in my mind, heart, and spirit that I was unlovable and was going to hell as a heathen.

My twenties and thirties were painful as my self-image propelled me to be with anyone who was willing to accept me. It was a dangerous scene. I got married at nineteen, pregnant, to an extremely abusive man, and we had two boys. Shortly after giving birth to the second child, I left the relationship but carried on in my same broken pattern, with some boyfriends being better than others.

It took me twenty years after high-school graduation to entertain the idea of studying to acquire my bachelor of social work, a program I failed in a spectacular fashion. In the first semester I did very well, attaining a B+ average, and started to think that maybe I wasn't an idiot after all. But old habits are stubborn and success just wasn't something that I could accept. My patterns of self-destruction continued, which led to me finishing my third semester with a 1.1 grade point average.

But it was a pivotal point in my life. During my time at university, I met an incredible individual, Theresa Neel. She was the Resident Elder at the university. Theresa took me under her wing, helping me to apply for my Indian status and for tuition funding, and taking me to cultural events throughout the Fraser Valley. This was my first introduction to my Indigenous heritage, a side that had not only been denied my whole life but ridiculed and shamed, and now I was learning to celebrate it and I was starting to belong somewhere.

Outside of school we travelled to traditional Indigenous events and my spirit soared. I finally had a place to belong. For the first time I wasn't terrified. As I trusted and grew to be trusted, I grew as a human being, participating wholeheartedly, and became a respected member of the community.

This is what the psychologist Martin Brokenleg speaks to in his teaching the Circle of Courage. In his book *The Science of Raising Courageous Kids*, he writes that belonging is necessary as the first basic human need (followed by mastery, independence, and generosity). I gain my strength and love from attending Indigenous ceremonies. In particular, adopting the teaching to the best of my ability that we are always in ceremony, that is, we are always in direct connection with the Creator, co-creating our lives.

Ongoing business, family, and health challenges

After I left university, I picked up a few jobs in the social work field but again nothing really stuck. Then tragedy struck. My eldest son died and my younger son went into foster care. I was a mess for years after and it really is a blur. The family pattern of our kids being in foster care was to continue for another generation. Sometime later I met my second husband and started putting my life back together.

I built a series of businesses to varying degrees of success, but nothing that ever really took off. What I did learn was that apparently I was never one to fear trying something new and that I have a strong entrepreneurial side. Who knew?

During this time my husband was diagnosed with stage 4 bladder cancer and given months to live. We were in shock but determined to live fully despite his disease. We were just returning from Hawaii, where Theresa and I had presented at an international conference for Indigenous educators, with my husband and two friends in tow. We had been a spectacular success.

As we were busy picking up our vehicle, I received a frantic call from my daughter-in-law that the Ministry of Children and

Family Development was coming to apprehend my young grandson. I rushed home, repacked my suitcase, and without a second thought hit the road, driving twelve hours to pick him up. As I was loading the truck with his belongings, two social workers showed up, and I let them know that I was taking custody of my grandson. To say the least, they were very confused and did not have much to say as I drove off. I had made a commitment on the way there that no one from my bloodline would ever be in the foster care system again, and my grandson has been with me and my husband ever since. My husband surpassed all the doctors' expectations, surviving his cancer, and has been an amazing stay-at-home dad to our grandson, who is now in high school and is thriving.

> *I examined my thoughts, read ferociously, and meditated continually, recalling my teachings, suspecting that if I wanted to relate to life differently, I would have to find a new way of seeing the world and myself.*

As I continued in the business world, I struggled with the competitive, self-centred mindset. It shredded my being like a cheese grater, yet I persevered for over five years. I mean, that's what all the business coaches say to do, and they must know better, right? So I carried on, leading myself right into a full-fledged mental breakdown, sitting in my backyard for two and a half years, not leaving the house, filled with anxiety and medication, with the words "Get off your butt and get to hustling" continuously ringing in my head.

Mine was not an easy journey, but at some point I was able to gain the perspective that if I had been in a train wreck and had broken every bone in my body, no one would be at me to pull myself up by my bootstraps and get back into life. But when you have mental health challenges, that is exactly the advice you get inundated with from all directions. It was at this moment that I realized what a gift of time this could be. I had the opportunity to completely recreate myself. I had nothing to go back to. I had no idea what my future could be. I examined my thoughts, read ferociously, and meditated continually, recalling my teachings, suspecting that if I wanted to relate to life differently, I would have to find a new way of seeing the world and myself. As I kept to myself, meditated, and talked with the Creator, eventually I was able to get to a place where I sought out help and attended group therapies at the local hospital. I was fifty when I was diagnosed with bipolar disorder.

I was done with the typical self-help books and was now reading the amazing array of Indigenous authors available. There were many books, chapters, paragraphs, and even sentences that I read and reread and reread yet again. I am so grateful to all of the authors who helped me through this time as I have never felt so alone, yet I felt myself coming to a place of rebirth. Finally, I was ready to rejoin the human race, but where to start? I wasn't ready to go to work, but I needed a stepping stone to get me out of the house. I made an agreement with myself that I would be open to whatever the Creator put in my path.

A new opportunity in the school system

One day my grandson came home from school with a notice asking for volunteers at his elementary school to help prep work for the teachers. *Great, no kids involved there, that will work. I could be open to that.* Did I mention that I don't enjoy kids? Through this group of volunteers, others saw that I had gifts to offer, and I was hired as an Indigenous Elder for a community program. I may not have any confidence in myself, but I know I can share the teachings that I have been blessed to receive. Again, my focus would be on the caregivers, no children interactions necessary— perfect. As the contract came to an end, my co-worker put my name forward for a position with the school district, working with Indigenous students. I had no idea what the job entailed but got hired and started at my first school. I was willing to give it a try.

As I started my career in the elementary schools, I found myself so very uncomfortable. Not because I was Indigenous. Not because I felt I had no idea what I was supposed to be doing. Not because my peers were better equipped than I was. I felt at odds because playing was extremely uncomfortable for me. Play is the language of children, and somehow I never learned how and I didn't want to. I spent four years working in elementary and am now in my second year at a high school, learning and growing alongside my students every day.

Early in my career, I was asked to drum and sing for Indigenous Peoples' Day at the elementary school. It was the first time I wore my cedar hat and button vest to a school. I was terrified, triggering the feelings I had in school as a child. With the help of my peers, I accomplished my first ceremony.

The ceremony was greatly appreciated by all, and I have gone on to do many performances within the school district and community. The first time I ever told my story in public was at a march for Orange Shirt Day organized by the school district at a local park, in front of hundreds of people. I was so blessed to have my husband and grandson stand in support and receive me afterwards to sob and smudge.

Students at my first elementary school entered a national Indigenous math contest and came in the top 10 overall. For

> *In Indigenous cultures, creating relationships and reciprocity is a priority. Regardless of your title or position, I am going to introduce myself and let you know what I have to offer . . .*

weeks I couldn't figure out what was wrong with me. My anxiety was through the roof and only added to my confusion, until I finally sat in my backyard, had a good cry, and took time to reflect. I realized that I was so, so proud of the work we had done but I had never allowed myself to ever feel proud and I needed to give myself permission to do so. *Hmm, emotional intelligence is a thing!*

During my first years in the school system as an Indigenous Support Worker, I received many requests from teachers for insights and information regarding Indigenous Peoples that I had no knowledge of. So, I decided to seek out this information and study Canadian-Indigenous relations from pre-Confederation to the present day. Now I direct others to resources, of which there is no shortage. Typically, I start them off with *Speaking Our Truth: A Journey of Reconciliation*, by Monique Gray Smith. I delved into deeper topics. Now, don't mislabel me—I am no scholar or expert in any area, but the more I learned, the more I was driven to understand, and the more I understood, the angrier I got. During this time, I recognized that the hatred of my childhood had been racism, causing me to leave home feeling completely unlovable, because all I felt was the hatred. Lately I am learning how many secrets there are in my family, in the history books, and in the country's relationship with Indigenous Peoples, and I continue to be hurt and angry.

As a child of the Sixties Scoop, I was a targeted racial group that was supposed to be eradicated through genocidal practices of the Canadian government. And to me, that makes it personal! The pain and the damage that I and so many others suffer is a direct result of these practices. Now, I don't want to get into all the many forms of genocide used in this country, because that in itself divides my people. We must all come together to heal, for healing takes place at a community level, not an individual level. Indigenous Peoples are not products of day school, residential school, or for that matter the Sixties Scoop and Millennial Scoop. We are all suffering from genocidal practices that continue to this day. Why else would we still have so many communities with no clean water, without infrastructure, and suffering from multiple other injustices? So go ahead, tell me to get over it! My greatest victory is that I am still here and I am for the most part healthy mentally, physically, emotionally, and spiritually, just as our Medicine Wheel teaches us to be. That gives me strength to be a fearless spiritual warrior. And it is this warrior that shows up for my students.

One thing I have learned to do well is to network. It is in my blood. In Indigenous cultures, creating relationships and reciprocity is a priority. Regardless of your title or position, I am going to introduce myself and let you know what I have to offer, and sometimes that is the tricky part to figure out. Usually, I get an answer from asking questions. People love to be asked for their opinions. Followed by intense listening, this approach creates a safe space for others to be open, vulnerable, and speak their truth. That is where connection lives, and connections based on trust are a necessity for human joy. Surround yourself with people whose qualities *you* wish to create within yourself.

Another lesson I learned is to slow down and be in the moment. In mainstream society we ask each other "How are you doing?" and invariably the answer is "I am so busy." We wear our busyness like a badge of honour. I much prefer to be asked how I am being so that I can be great, wonderful, fabulous. I refuse to be busy. I have alarms on my phone that remind me to check in on how I am *being*, because we must put our focus on what is most important to us. As one of my Elders says, "We are human beings, not human doings."

Every step I take, I am either striving or failing forward. I continue to be a ferocious reader, especially on implementing Indigenous ways of being and learning in the classroom, such as Ensouling Our Schools (see the guide at eos_teachers_manual_final.pdf). I attend many training opportunities to grow as a human being and be of further service to my community, which continues to grow.

I also am always scanning for opportunities to learn, whether Indigenous or not. This creates an opportunity for me to act as a bridge where possible. At a recent leadership session, Abbotsford district superintendent Sean Nosak shared with us his blog "30 Years. 30 Lessons." I always find a golden nugget in shares like these, learning from other's experiences, successes, and mistakes—celebrating that person's willingness to be vulnerable.

As I do my decolonizing work in the school system, I am decolonizing myself. And this will be a lifelong journey. As I explore my personal history, there are many secrets I have uncovered that I have had to cope with. For example, my name isn't Tina, my birthday on my records is incorrect, and I recently discovered that the story of my birth mother dying from passing out while drunk is a lie.

I was born Flora after my maternal Haida nonni ("grandmother"). One of my older sisters that I have reconnected with who was in charge of caring for me and my siblings as babies informs me that I was born in the spring, not November. And my brother recently said that my birth mother was actually murdered and is one of the Missing and Murdered Indigenous Women and Girls.

Reflecting on all of this, I have decided to legally change my name back to Flora and take the middle name Joy after my birth mother, Joyce. This is my starting place on my journey of Joy. Living in truth as best I can and being a truth teller. Building a firm foundation based on love and support from which I can do the work I am called to do in the schools, in the community, and wherever else this journey takes me. Who would ever have guessed? As for working with the kids, okay, they are pretty cool too.

FLORA JOY LAKEY

Flora is a proud member of the Haida Nation currently residing in the Fraser Valley with her husband, grandson, and niece. Flora has faced many obstacles in her life yet continues to strive to make our communities a better place for all. Rooted in traditional teachings, Flora works in the school district uplifting Indigenous students, allowing them to participate in traditional practices. In the community Flora sits on boards for cultural non-profit organizations and participates in traditional cultural events, bringing laughter and joy everywhere she goes.

🌐 FloraJoy.ca

FROM MY FIRST BREATH
BY MARILYN R. WILSON

If you are struggling with feeling out of step with those around you, know you are not alone. Simply choose to live each day as honestly and authentically as you can.

THE MONTHS LEADING UP TO WRITING this chapter held a lot of aha moments. Several of the books I read shared experiences that landed hard. One in particular stands out. The author was attending a personal empowerment weekend event run by a highly respected speaker. He was there incognito doing research for his book. While I was reading about the rah-rah environment and over-the-top manipulation to buy he saw happening, I felt my anxiety soar. I had to put the book down. When I picked it up again, I realized I still hadn't processed why I reacted so strongly, so decided to skip ahead to the next chapter.

Understanding finally arrived during a phone call with my youngest brother that unexpectedly turned serious. I mentioned how I had become triggered when reading that book, and my comment opened the door for a long-overdue conversation reflecting on our shared childhood memories. I finally realized the universe had been speaking to me, trying to let me know about hidden, dark matter deep within that still needed to be unearthed and healed.

Over the past decade I had made a conscious effort to work on personal growth and self-acceptance, releasing the baggage from my early years and embracing the truth that I was not broken. I truly believed I had finished cleaning out the cobwebs. As far as I was concerned, my childhood had been explored, accepted, released, and lessons internalized, so this guidance came as a surprise.

I was not mistreated or unloved as a child. I experienced no physical abuse, my parents stayed together happily, there was always a roof over our heads and food on the table, and no one abused alcohol or used drugs. I simply did not fit into the expectations that surrounded me. However, what I was now experiencing seemed to indicate there was something—or some things—unresolved, still to be discovered. The signs of trauma response were clearly there, but they floated without anchor. I was confused.

During the phone call with my brother, I caught a glimpse of our childhood through his eyes. We grew up in the late 1950s to mid-1960s in a small town in America's Midwest. We had one television station, no exposure to the world outside our bubble, and religion was taken very seriously. Our father was a minister, which meant we also lived in the public eye. Added to that was society's limited vision of what the roles of men, women, and children should be. We were small kids carrying the heavy weight of societal expectations on our shoulders.

How we coped was wildly different. Both my brothers seemed to thrive. They were quiet, appeared content, and drew no negative attention. I was not like that and found myself very jealous as a result. How did they manage to fit in so well? How did everyone around me seem to fit in so well? No matter how much I craved to be accepted for who I was, the truth was, it just wasn't going to happen. My failure to conform brought feelings of anger and deep shame. I accepted what I heard from others—that I was broken.

As my brother shared his memories, I was floored to learn he had struggled every bit as much as I had. His coping skill was to bury his pain deep and pretend to fit in. While I wanted to be him, he wanted to be me. He thought I was brave to stand up for myself as I did. He in turn was surprised to learn I never *was* standing up for myself; I simply couldn't pretend to be someone I was not. Here we were, two siblings in our sixties, only now discovering how flawed our memories were.

It's hard to describe growing up in that era to those who have always had global access to others through the internet, social media, podcasts, and hundreds of TV stations. Our isolation from anything different kept us ignorant and under control. Today our social bubble is no longer our single source of truth. Information on the world's many diverse lifestyles, beliefs, and traditions is easily accessible. As I child I could never imagine one day I would be immersed in a world filled with such variety.

As I look back on my early years, being tightly bound is exactly how it felt. I began trying to break those bindings from the moment I was born . . .

As I reflect on what I have learned over the last couple of months, I feel people come to defy social expectations in one of two ways. The first is by choice. We choose to defy social expectations because of personal growth, the acceptance of new ideas, life challenges, or even an aha moment. An example would be becoming a vegan. So many paths could inspire this—animal rights, health issues, or a desire to eat more sustainably. Any life choice that stands out as weird or wrong to your social grouping would serve as an example. This choice is usually made at an age when you are in control of your life.

The other path to defying social expectations is simply to be born to this journey. From your first breath, the very essence of who you are sets you apart from the societal expectations that surround you. I know this reality intimately and can share from personal experience it is not an easy path. As a young person I wished desperately to fit in, but didn't seem to have the ability to do that. In despair, I dimmed my inner light and did my best to fade into the background. This tactic did not work well, but it was my only defence.

I love a quote I read recently by American author Sarah J. Maas. "It's okay to be different, to stand out, to break the rules that bind you." The imagery of breaking out of the bindings placed on me hits home. As I look back on my early years, being tightly bound is exactly how it felt. I began trying to break those bindings from the moment I was born, without even realizing it, and have spent a lifetime working to free myself.

All through high school I was out of sync with other students. I didn't care about dating, sports, proms, and fashion. My soul was drawn to the world stage—the Vietnam War, the outing of Billie Jean King, poverty, racism, world hunger. I am grateful for the three beautiful friends that embraced me as I was. But even with their support, I chose to graduate a year early and leave for a university more than four hundred miles away a few months later. I needed a new beginning.

Away from home, my inner self worked frantically to build a hard protective shell around my heart. I still struggled to make friends as I seemed to not only walk through life differently but also see the world differently. And I was sure no one would like me if they saw my flaws. It wasn't until I was in my late thirties and a mother with kids in elementary school I realized my racing mind and intensity had a name—attention deficit disorder (ADD). Other people I met actually did not experience life the same way I did. But instead of bringing a sense of relief, this knowledge was just one more flaw that set me apart.

As I began to walk through each day living as honestly as I could, I began to experience positive shifts. One of the best was a change in my relationship with women.

There was a single moment around the time I turned thirty when I began to embrace who I was openly. My father had passed. I was talking on the phone to my mother, who was still deeply religious. For a while we shared what was happening in our lives, and what my brothers and relatives were all up to. Then somehow the big *R* arose—religion. I always avoided that subject as best I could, and just quietly listened when I couldn't. This time would be different.

I no longer remember exactly what triggered my honesty, but it felt like the right time for some long-overdue clarity on my part. With firm determination, but as lovingly and simply as I could, I began, "Mom, I do not believe in God the way you do, nor do I believe in heaven or hell. I am no longer a teenager. I am thirty years old. I am not rebelling and I will not grow out of this stage. This is who I am." She began to cry and hung up, which broke my heart.

I never wanted to hurt my mom or challenge the beliefs that filled her with joy. However, after the call was over I felt lighter, like a heavy burden had fallen away. This stands out as my first step towards acknowledging that I was not broken or failing. I was on the path I was born to embrace. My uniqueness was my strength. Cracking open that protective shell to let the world see my authentic self was the only way to become who I was born to be. Confronting my mother was also my first step towards self-acceptance.

I doubt my mother saw it this way, but I feel this was when our relationship shifted from mother-child to an adult one. As our old patterns faded and we were more honest in our conversations, our broken bond began to heal. Although she never did come to accept my spiritual beliefs, we built an honest connection that deepened when I became a mother. I was full of sorrow when she passed and missed our regular catch-up phone calls.

As an adult, the issues I chose to support and the truths I fought for usually represented a challenge to the status quo. I began to realize there was a deep resistance to change in society. A simple example: I did not change my last name when I married. I just couldn't see any reason to change it. My husband was fully supportive, but my mother and other relatives were upset. Not only did they not approve, they also were distraught over how to address mail to us. Some chose to write Glen and Marilyn without a last name, while others addressed their mail to Mr. and Mrs. Glen Anderson. The last felt hurtful but they were family, so I chose not to make an issue of it.

At the age of fifty my outlook began to shift. I still struggled with feeling out of step, but that began to change when an opportunity opened for me to interview and write articles for a New York magazine. It took doing over 150 interviews before I realized the impact those stories were having on me. Listening to people's individual journeys made me aware of how beautifully diverse our paths could be. There was no right or wrong way to live or believe. It was okay to choose a different life. It was okay to be out of step.

What was even more astounding was, no one seemed to care whether they fit in. They were comfortable in their own skin. No life was perfect, but each person had found their purpose, and they didn't care if others disapproved. I finally understood I was exactly who I was meant to be and that my quirks were not flaws, they were my strengths. I wasn't rebelling or being difficult, I was simply becoming me. Defying social expectations was not an act of rebellion, it was the result of my living the life I was born to have.

As I began to walk through each day living as honestly as I could, I began to experience positive shifts. One of the best was a change in my relationship with women. Growing up with brothers, with a mother who envisioned I would be an obedient "girly girl," and never being interested in the same things as the women around me, I just naturally gravitated towards male friendships. Men were not often given to subterfuge, and their expectations for me were ones I felt comfortable with.

One day while conducting an interview, I was exposed to the concept of co-operative economics: coming together as a village to raise everyone up equally. This struck a chord. Up to that moment I simply fell into friendships with people that surrounded me. I needed to build my village purposefully with those who wanted to work towards common goals. I was nervous exposing my authentic self to strangers—we don't shed a lifelong habit of hiding overnight—so I took baby steps as I moved outward into the world. What I quickly discovered was a whole community of amazing, powerful, wonderful women. They had been there all along.

One by one I worked to build strong friendships. My community is now filled with vibrant, inspiring women living unexpected lives and working to have a positive impact on the world. Some are artists, some entrepreneurs, and others have chosen unique paths. We support each other without competition and share our insights freely. These women inspire me, and I hope I inspire them.

Where am I at this point in my non-traditional journey? Over the past few years, ageism has become the newest social expectation to try to put me back in a box. It can be oh-so-subtle or quite blatant. A while back when someone questioned the appropriateness of a post I had made on social media, another person commented, "Marilyn is older and doesn't understand." I did understand. I clearly posted my intentions. I found this response insulting. There have been other instances of ageism, but that one stands out as one of the more upsetting.

As an act of defiance, I decided to make a bucket list. Its purpose was twofold—to help me avoid falling into a rut, and to help change how others see aging women. I have travelled, taken classes, ziplined, jumped out of a plane, climbed on a jungle gym with my granddaughter (which led to me perform a backwards somersault out of a tube), learned to write poetry, worn unexpected clothing, and taken to the stage to speak. I hope the effect of sharing these adventures will be to surprise and educate.

A few days ago I saw a great poster that said, "You are only young once, but you can be immature forever." While I don't believe staying young in mind and body means acting immature, that line brought a smile. I remember thinking my mom was old at fifty, and she embraced that notion fully. Now we see men and women over fifty wearing statement-making clothes, and they are out there still working, dancing, singing, acting, writing, and climbing Mount Everest. Thanks are owed to the brave seniors who choose to step out of the roles assigned them by society and rewrite the script for those who follow.

I want to close with a confession. The changes my body is going through as I age do make it harder to keep embracing new experiences. And the images of privileged, beautiful older women now being held up in the media as what the new 50, 60, or 70 looks like can be intimidating. I don't look that way. While this might change, right now I don't want to spend my time and money on expensive beauty treatments. I want to spend them travelling, having new adventures, and trying new things. I do have one role model to hang onto—British actor Judi Dench, who embraces aging naturally without apology. I hope to meet her one day and say thanks.

I love what American musician David Grohl shared in his book *The Storyteller*. He talked about wanting to experience life to the fullest, wildly exploring, seeking adventures, and pushing himself to the limits. And if that meant skidding in at the end looking a little used and worn, he was okay with that. Me too! I want to skid in at the end of my life looking totally worn out, completely exhausted, with a big smile on my face, and shouting, "Now, that was a blast!" I may change my mind about those wrinkles in the future, but I hope not.

If you are struggling with feeling out of step with those around you, know you are not alone. Simply choose to live each day as honestly and authentically as you can. Mute the chaotic voices surrounding you so you can hear your heart speak. And let the rest of the world take care of itself.

MARILYN R. WILSON

Marilyn is a freelance writer, published author, speaker, and poet with a passion for sharing the stories of others. Her career began in an unusual way—when she answered a Craigslist ad for which she had no qualifications. Somehow she made the cut and quickly discovered a deep passion for hearing others share their unique stories. Over the next seventeen years she conducted over 200 interviews, was co-owner of a magazine, and was published in others. In 2015 she launched her first book, *Life Outside the Box*, followed in 2018 by *The Wisdom of Listening*.

Whether through a random encounter or a scheduled interview, her goal is the same—to give wings to the stories of inspiring individuals, and to pass on the wisdom shared with her in interviews and discovered during her own life journey.

marilynrwilson.com

marilynrwilson_official

MarilynRWilsonWriter

marilynwilson8752

YOUR STORY IS YOUR CHOICE
BY SAMANTHA DAY

My life story and my unique purpose cannot be separated. It took all of these challenges and life adventures to bring me to a place of knowing who I serve and how I can serve them.

EVERY DAY WE MAKE A CHOICE. We choose how we want to live and how we are going to see the challenges we are dealing with. We can choose to see what seems "hard" as a struggle, or we can see the situation as a teacher. We choose what we focus on and how we want to show up for ourselves and others: what truths we want to accept and make our own, and those that aren't for us. Every day, we can choose to find and feel the joy, no matter what life is throwing at us.

I started learning this lesson at six years old and must be hard-headed, since I've had to relearn it a few more times for good measure. Through multiple health and life challenges, both my own and of those close to me, my mettle and my ability to choose how to move through this journey and to find the joy and fun have been tested and honed to a fine skill.

On a podcast I listened to recently, they talked about having a "message on their heart." This phrase really hit home for me. I have always felt an internal pressure to do something big or different with my life. I've always known that something had to do with adventure and helping people. So I had the logical plan of becoming a doctor. Help people. *Check.* Get to learn and know about a lot of stuff. *Check.* Get to ask questions and solve problems. *Check.* I am someone who is curious, loves adventure and shared experiences. Working for Doctors Without Borders would check those boxes too. I had a plan. But as you likely know, life often has other plans for us, and it sure did for me.

The first time life tried to get this message through my hard head was when I was six years old. I fell off a playground apparatus and ruptured a kidney. I'm told it was touch and go whether I would make it for about a week. This may have been one of the best things that ever happened to me. The experience taught me lessons that I have carried with me and used so many times in life. I now knew without a doubt that my parents loved me. While in the hospital I learned to find joy in a difficult or sad situation. My roommate died of leukemia shortly after my stay, but while I was there we made the absolute most fun out of our time together.

Healing from my ruptured kidney was a long road. I learned how to listen to my body and the limits it was setting (mostly). I was six, after all, and Hula Hooping looked like so much fun! I learned to heal from a major injury, deal with chronic pain, and, perhaps most importantly, learned how not to be defined and limited by a significant trauma. To choose how I wanted to literally move through the world and how I wanted my story to be told. Bonus: I won every contest of kids asking "Who's had the biggest injury?"

The lessons and coping skills I had learned helped me when my mother was diagnosed with cancer. She died when I was sixteen and suddenly my path wasn't clear anymore. I already knew that there is no time guaranteed to us, having ruptured a kidney as a kid, but this knowledge really sank in as my mother was dying. It became crystal clear to me that I had chosen "Doctor" because it checked the expected boxes and equally clear to me that there was a large piece of something meaningful missing if I went in that direction. So I decided to let go of having a plan and listen to what my gut told me. Following my intuition wasn't easy and it was lonely at times. I heard a lot of "You're wasting your potential." I spent a few years after high school directionless, waiting for inspiration—not a state I'm willing to stay in for long.

At twenty-one, inspiration hadn't struck and I decided that I needed to acquire some sort of post-secondary education. I knew I wanted a short-term career that would give me freedom to have adventures, that would enable me to help people, that didn't require a PhD or master's degree, and that would still be a step forward if I decided to go to university later. I'm pretty proud of how I ended up choosing a path. I made a list of what an ideal day, week, year would look like and knew that the career I was seeking had to be a job with autonomy. I shared the list with my RMT at the time and she suggested becoming a registered massage therapist since it checked all of the boxes. I applied and two weeks later I was a full-time student.

Being a registered massage therapist was great! I was living my adventure, could travel and experience life while helping people. I got jobs with benefits I wanted, like golfing at a fancy course and heli-skiing. Best job perk ever. I even had a job in the Mediterranean on a private yacht lined up. I knew I wasn't going to be an RMT for the long haul but still didn't know what I truly wanted to be doing. I still had this feeling deep inside that I wasn't where I was meant to be.

An unplanned fork in the road

I was waiting for the path to present itself and chalking up life experiences on the way. Sam version 1.0 appreciated life and went after what she wanted. She was living in alignment with herself and her goals and finding joy wherever possible. I am proud of that version of myself. It's taken me almost fifteen years to get back to a similar inner feeling that I had then. Because at age twenty-four, I was hit by a truck. And not the metaphorical kind—the F-350 long bed extended cab kind. I don't remember it or most of the time I was in the ICU, blessings of a head injury. I came through the accident with broken bones, torn muscles, nerve damage, and a moderate brain bleed. This was a very unplanned fork in the road. But I was incredibly lucky. I'm not sure what the statistics are, but I know that getting hit head-on at highway speeds by a much larger vehicle isn't something you want to sign up for.

This theme of incredible luck as I go through challenges is a recurring one in my life. I believe we always have a choice in how to feel and think about circumstances, and I have had the ability since I was a child to choose to see the spark of light or joy and focus on that as a way to shift the fear and grief. Make your life purposeful and celebrate it.

I wasn't the same me after the accident, and I found myself going through the grief process and mourning the person I had been. I was changed by what happened in ways that I still feel all the time and that others don't always see. My brain injury was mostly damage to my prefrontal cortex, the executive centre of the brain. This affected my short-term memory and ability to multi-task, regulate myself emotionally, and filter myself verbally, among many other things. For someone who had aspirations of being a doctor or type of professional that required a PhD, with focus and good executive brain functions, this wasn't ideal.

> I listened to other people's expectations of me that suggested I look at new jobs that wouldn't overtax me, expect too much of me, or be overwhelming.

Enter a decade plus of feeling lost. For a long time, I focused on my limitations. There's a quote by the novelist, philosopher, and artist Kelly Lee Phipps that starts: "If you argue for your limitations you get to keep them." And this is what I unknowingly did. (The quote continues: "But if you argue for your possibilities you get to create them!"—something I live by now.) At the time, while I did great personal work around my mindset, outlook on life, gratitude, and appreciation, I also stayed stuck because of the thought *I can't do that anymore*. I had chosen to ignore some of the limitations set by the specialists, but others I really clung to. And I listened to other people's expectations of me that suggested I look at new jobs that wouldn't overtax me, expect too much of me, or be overwhelming. In essence, jobs that felt boring. So I kept working as an RMT, because even though performing my job hurt physically, it was worth it for the autonomy, freedom, and meaningful impact I could make on patients.

By thinking about all the things I was limited in, I wasn't seeing all the things I could do. This is when the lesson of choosing my story kicked in again. In the words of life cycle celebrant Lise Leroux, "I needed direction in my life and a positive marker." I had realized by now that working for myself was a top priority. The ability to manage my schedule and go through my days in a way that worked for my brain became number one on the list while I

> *Success to me means having the freedom of time to spend with my family, go on adventures, give to others, and be curious and authentically me.*

considered new careers. That, and having a sense of direction and purpose in my career and life would give me a positive goal to focus on. I started on an intentional search to find people who had similar injuries and were successful entrepreneurs. I had decided to seek out and surround myself with information and stories of other people with traumatic brain injuries who had chosen to create their own story of success and fulfillment. Why reinvent the wheel?

A new direction through yet more challenges

I'll stop and define my version of success here. Success to me means having the freedom of time to spend with my family, go on adventures, give to others, and be curious and authentically me. Deciding that I got to choose my story felt like a new chapter.

I knew I wanted a new career. As much as doing massage was good for my brain, it was hard on my body and injuries. I started doing photography because it brought me joy; I always had a creative pursuit to look forward to. I also re-evaluated how I felt about being told I shouldn't have kids, because this would be too much for me to handle mentally. I took stock of what mattered to me, what I truly wanted, and what sacrifices I was willing to make to get there. I decided that I did want kids and no matter the challenge, I would find a way.

The saying "Be careful what you wish for, you just might get it" applies here. Having kids *was* a challenge. I couldn't get pregnant and again, my ability to find the joy and choose how I went through the challenge was tested. Was I happy and joyful every day? Nope. There were many moments and days of sadness, grief, and depression. Yet I would always get back to a place of choosing to find something positive to focus on. I could be happy for a friend who did get pregnant or appreciate the free time I had, since I didn't have a baby yet.

After four, perhaps six years of trying (that time is a bit of a blur), my partner and I did IVF. I just *knew* it would work. I had a hypnotherapist work with me, I did affirmations—you name it, it was part of my mental routine. And we have two beautiful, healthy children. Having them was so hard and yet so worth it. Anyone who has gone through fertility challenges will know about the mental and physical toll. How it can feel lonely since not too many people talk about their experience with infertility.

I started to feel like my purpose and life were coming together, despite how hard having children is. And I did find caring for (never mind birthing) a baby hard. I was absolutely exhausted. More than I had been after the head injury. That's when I found out that I had a serious congenital heart defect.

I had known for years that there was something wrong with me. My symptoms were explained away as the result of my other injuries. For example, my headaches were linked to the injuries to my neck and spine when I ruptured my kidney and later was in the motor vehicle accident. Shortness of breath was attributed to not being active enough after injuries; just slightly high blood pressure was "white coat syndrome." The list goes on.

I was working on getting a referral to a cardiologist when my face and hand suddenly went numb. It was the best thing that could have happened. A stroke didn't seem likely, but let's not mess around here, so off to the hospital I went. The paramedic with me in the ambulance commented that sometimes these weird things happen so that the bigger issue can be found. Boy, was he right.

Again, I was incredibly lucky that the doctors found out what the issue was. The narrowing (coarctation) of my aorta was quite significant and I was at risk of an aortic dissection, an inner tear—and of the aorta tearing off the heart. Definitely not good. It was terrifying. I didn't want my children to lose their mom, knowing how hard that is. And for the first time in my health journey, I was *mad*. I found out that medical staff had done an echocardiogram because of my broken sternum after my car accident and the coarctation of my aorta was in that echo report. *And no one had told me.* Capital M-A-D mad.

This experience was a massive test of my ability to choose how I go through a challenge. The year-long wait to see a specialist and have the issue corrected was stressful. And I have PTSD from the stent procedure, where I felt it all and my aorta was torn. I struggled to be present and joyful during this time but am so grateful for the supportive and caring people in my life.

I have spent so much of my life in my own head. Thinking about *What am I thinking?*, considering the options that are open to me, questioning my decisions, and *Is it the right one?* Not really knowing who I am anymore and feeling lost in my life purpose. The whole time knowing I want to help others in some way and beating myself up that I'm not using what I have learned from these challenges to do that. *Surely* I've had enough growth and perspective to find a way to give back.

The blessing that has come from the ruptured kidney, the loss of my mother, the head injury, IVF, all the other "life stuff" and finally the coarctation is that I now have direction for my sense of purpose. My life story and my unique purpose cannot be separated. It took all of these challenges and life adventures to bring me to a place of knowing who I serve and how I can serve them. I have the ability to show people how beautiful their life is, even when it's hard, and that is a gift I am honoured to give. Documenting life and families in an authentic and meaningful way through photography and coaching others through their life's adventure is the true gift of my life challenges.

My story could be one of only sadness and loss, depression and PTSD, pain and suffering, the story of a victim. I could accept the limitations that others perceive someone in my circumstances has and accept their social expectations. But these are all just experiences I have or am going through. They are not my whole story. My story is one of joy, personal growth, and choosing to be happy no matter what. Of defying those social expectations.

I choose to focus on what I can change and where I can make a meaningful impact. Both for myself and for others. My route to this place hasn't always been easy, and I have become a great problem-solver to move through these challenges in a way that brings me fulfillment and joy. And it's no secret: you too can find joy and purpose, by knowing what you value and choosing to bring that knowledge into your life every single damn day. I value joy, curiosity, adventure, love, authenticity, and personal growth. What matters to you?

SAMANTHA DAY

Samantha grew up in BC's Okanagan (Oyama is the best!) and resides there with her husband and two children, exploring the many exciting and scenic locations in the valley. Her parents had film cameras that recorded all their family adventures— camping road trips, canoe trips, Scout camps—and everyday life. She is now the keeper of the family photo albums, and her favourite photos are the ones that capture her family's personalities and interactions.

As a professional photographer, whether she is making images for a business, documenting a family story, or capturing one of life's many adventures, Samantha's first thought is always *How can I make this experience as natural and stress-free as possible?*

Some random facts: Samantha is happiest when she is outdoors on an adventure with people she cares about.

She loves a good road trip where random stops can and do happen, and she likes to save the last pickle in the jar.

🌐 samanthaday.ca
📷 samanthadayphotography
f samanthadayphotography

HONOURING OUR TRUE SELVES
BY RINO MURATA

Defying social expectations isn't about rebellion; it's about self-discovery. It's about realizing that the expectations placed upon us were never truly ours to begin with.

IF I DIDN'T KNOW ANYTHING about expectations, I wouldn't know who I am. Part of me thinks I'd be lazy, sitting on the couch watching TV all day. If I didn't have any expectations for myself, instead of working for a statistical software company right after college, I would have opted to study and travel abroad. My outfits wouldn't be so conservative; I'd probably choose clothes that were more tight-fitting. But are these my true desires, or are they just fantasies because they're the opposite of my current reality? I'm not sure.

Expectations shape every aspect of our lives, often without us even realizing it. From a young age, we're groomed to meet standards set by others—our parents, teachers, peers, and society. These expectations guide our choices, influence our self-perception, and mould our futures. But what happens when these imposed expectations clash with what we truly want?

The bar was set high for me at age four when I started babysitting my one-year-old sister. Changing diapers, feeding her, staying home alone with her—these things came naturally to me. It sounds crazy, but I learned to do them because I had to. The line between our authentic selves and the selves shaped by expectations isn't as clear as we'd like to believe. That line is so fuzzy that we may never fully know where it lies because we can't completely separate who we are from the collective influences around us.

To explore this further, I sat down with my journal and created two lists. In the first list, I wrote down what is important to my authentic self—words such as "compassion," "understanding," "relationships," "integrity," and "love." In the second list, I wrote down actions that I felt were shaped by expectations: "be proper," "dress well," "get educated," "marry well," and "have good manners."

> **We become adults without fully understanding who we really are, and when that manufactured self is all we've ever known, breaking free from that bondage is a painful experience.**

It didn't take long to see that my true self also valued some of what my expected self had become. My parents expected me to go to a good university, and I did. But I love learning anyway, to the point where getting certifications has become a bit of an obsession. I always wanted to get married, and it was expected of me, so I married my first husband at age twenty-three because I was afraid of being left behind. I never questioned the need to become a "good" housewife.

Having my first son at twenty-six seemed like the natural next step after getting married. Having two more boys before turning thirty-one, I expected nothing less than to be a good mom to them. And yet, despite doing all the things I would have done anyway, so many things went wrong.

When expectations are set by others, we often feel we have to conform to someone else's standards, whether they themselves have met those standards or not. Expectations go wrong when they're based on desires, not reality. Like when I expected my dyslexic son to pick up reading as easily as I had. No one had taught me to read, so why shouldn't reading come naturally to him? It's not like I was exceptionally smart.

There's another way in which expectations go wrong: wrong assumptions. My self-worth and confidence had always been low, because I looked for external validation, yet no one would have guessed that I did. So if someone like me could learn to read, why couldn't anyone? This cycle of setting wrong standards, unrealistic expectations, and miscalculations sets everyone up for disappointment. How about resentment? Anyone?

Then why do I get such a kick out of pressure—taking an exam, getting married twice, and being confident that I'm a good mom—when those same things drove me to burnout, followed by a two-year depression after getting into college, going through a divorce despite doing everything right, and watching my kids struggle despite doing all the things a good mom would?

It's because those actions lacked ownership—they were dictated by someone else's timeline. Expectations become crippling when we lose agency, when they force us to follow a timeline that isn't ours, out of fear of disapproval. Defying expectations goes against our deep-rooted fear of abandonment because no one can survive alone. For some, living in our truth means being disowned. For others, it might mean burying our true selves to conform and be accepted. We become adults without fully understanding who we really are, and when that manufactured self is all we've ever known, breaking free from that bondage is a painful experience.

Yet, even though the manufactured part of me is so deeply ingrained—so much so that how I dress seems to be part of who I am—I sometimes fantasize about how things would be if I could break free from those expectations. It's the allure of freedom, the idea of shedding those layers that were never truly mine, that seems so enticing. But I realize now that it's not about completely discarding what's been ingrained; it's about owning who I am, who I want to be, and having the agency to make those decisions for myself.

From conformity to authenticity

Our family's journey is a perfect example of how what seems like defiance from the outside was, in reality, a quest for authenticity and self-ownership. When I first became a mother, I followed the conventional path with my boys. They attended traditional schools, participated in the expected extracurricular activities, and followed the structured educational journey that most of us are familiar with.

But over time, I started to question whether this path was truly serving my neurodivergent children. I noticed how the rigid structure of conventional education didn't align with their individual learning styles or needs. The spark of curiosity that they naturally had as young children seemed to fade, become less visible under the demands of standardized tests, homework, and a one-size-fits-all curriculum. And most of all, their spark dimmed due to the pressure I myself was putting on my children, because of my need to conform and meet expectations.

So, we made a bold decision: I pulled my boys out of the traditional school system and began home-schooling them. It was a step that many saw as defiant, a rejection of the established educational norms. But for us, it was less about defiance and more about finding an educational approach that truly fit our family's values and my children's unique ways of learning.

Home-schooling eventually led us down the path to un-schooling—a shift that emphasizes child-led learning and trusts that children will naturally learn what they need to know when they are ready. This was a far cry from the conventional educational model I was raised with, and at first, it felt like a complete departure from everything I had ever known.

> *Even when we appear to be doing the same thing as everyone else, it's the presence of agency and ownership that makes all the difference.*

However, what became clear over time was that this journey wasn't about rejecting traditional education for the sake of being different. It was about creating an environment where my boys could thrive, where they could have agency and ownership over their learning that they had not had in a conventional school. Our journey was about honouring their individual needs and allowing them to explore their interests in a way that felt natural and meaningful to them.

After years of home-schooling and unschooling, my boys made the decision to return to public school. This time, though, it was on their terms. They had tasted the freedom of self-directed learning and understood the power of having control over their education. When they chose to re-enter the traditional school system, it wasn't because they were conforming to societal expectations; it was because they felt it was the right choice for them at that point in their lives.

This experience taught me a profound lesson: even when we appear to be doing the same thing as everyone else, it's the presence of agency and ownership that makes all the difference. When my boys returned to public school, it was with a new-found sense of confidence and autonomy. They weren't just following a path that was laid out for them; they were making a conscious decision to engage with that path in a way that worked for them.

From the outside, it might have looked like we were rebelling against the conventional education system, only to return to it later on. But in reality, we were finding what worked best for our family at different stages of our lives. Our journey was about giving my boys the freedom to choose their own path, whether that meant unschooling at home or rejoining the public school system.

This journey reinforced for me that true authenticity comes not from rejecting social and cultural norms for the sake of doing so, but rather from making choices that align with our deepest values and needs. It's about having the courage to diverge from the expected path when it no longer serves us and the wisdom to return to it when it does. Most importantly, it's about ensuring that whatever path we choose, we select it with full ownership and agency.

The illusion of defiance

When we think we're defying social expectations, we often imagine ourselves as rebels, standing against the tide of societal norms. But in reality, what's happening is something much more profound: we're simply coming into our true selves. The so-called defiance isn't a deliberate act of rebellion but rather an authentic expression of who we truly are, free from the constraints that have been imposed upon us.

It's from the outside—the perspective of others—that our actions appear defiant. To those who have known us only as the manufactured selves shaped by societal expectations, our journey towards authenticity can seem shocking or even rebellious. They see us stepping out of the roles we were once confined to, and in their eyes, this looks like a bold challenge to the status quo. But from our own perspective, it doesn't feel like defiance at all. It feels like coming home, like finding a part of ourselves that was lost or buried. It's a process of unearthing our true desires, values, and identities that had been hidden under layers of expectations. What others perceive as a sudden change is, for us, the gradual unveiling of our authentic selves.

It's important to recognize that what others see as defiance is often a projection of their own discomfort with change. When we step out of the roles we've been assigned, our behaviour can unsettle those who are still deeply entrenched in societal expectations. Our authenticity can be perceived as a threat because it challenges the norms that others may still be trying to uphold. But our journey towards authenticity is not about them— it's about us. It's about shedding the layers of who we were told to be and embracing who we actually are. It's about finding peace in our own skin, even if it means walking a path that others don't understand.

Defying social expectations isn't about rebellion; it's about self-discovery. It's about realizing that the expectations placed upon us were never truly ours to begin with. They were handed down to us, and we accepted them, often without question. But as we grow and evolve, we begin to see that these expectations don't fit who we really are. And so we let them go—not to defy society, but to honour ourselves.

This redefinition of defiance is crucial in understanding our own journey. The courage to live authentically is not a process of breaking the rules but a quest to rewrite them to reflect our own truths. We are creating a life that resonates with who we are at our core, rather than one that conforms to the expectations of others. When we embrace this perspective, we can approach our choices with less fear of judgment and more confidence in our own path. We can move forward, not as rebels without a cause, but as individuals with a deep sense of purpose and self-awareness. We're not defying the world—we're embracing ourselves.

In the end, what others see as defiance is simply the process of us becoming who we were always meant to be. It's a natural evolution, one that everyone experiences if they dare to look beyond the surface of societal expectations and dig into the depths of their own being.

As I reflect back, I realize that without those initial expectations, I might never have embarked on this journey of self-discovery. But now, having stepped into my authentic self, I understand that the real power lies not in defying expectations, but in living a life that's true to who I am. The journey is yours to navigate, and the most powerful thing you can do is stay true to who you are, regardless of what others may think. Living in alignment with your true self isn't about proving anything to anyone—it's about finding peace in your own authenticity. And to me, that is freedom.

RINO MURATA

Rino is a relationship coach who helps clients get their romantic relationships right by getting a clear understanding of themselves through a holistic body-mind-soul approach and emotional intelligence. Rino believes love and relationships are worth pursuing. She discovered through parenting her three sons that love itself cannot build a strong and healthy relationship, but being able to have mutual trust, honesty, and respect is what makes relationships meaningful to everyone involved.

A certified Integral Life Coach and certified Trauma-Informed coach, Rino holds a bachelor's degree in sociology from Sophia University in Tokyo. When she is not working or furthering her training to be a better coach, Rino enjoys cooking for her blended family with five kids or zoning out in front of the TV, not remembering until the very last moment the show she is watching for the third time.

🌐 rinomurata.com

📧 rino@rinomurata.com

LETTING GO WITH GRACE
BY JAZ GILL

As we grow and evolve in life, many people, places, and things will be given to us and taken away. It is important to have the ability to flow in the receiving and the letting go.

THIS IS A STORY ABOUT LETTING GO with grace and holding on with hope. There are times in our life that we lose a lot and we have to let go of a lot. These times are full of heartache and heartbreak. But through the grace of a compassionate Universe, we are given all we need to rebuild and become stronger and better. We owe this to ourselves and to our loved ones. With the work, effort, and time we invest in our healing, we are gifted with the beautiful reward of priceless inner peace.

I was born in Northern India. I came to British Columbia, Canada, when I was five years old, the youngest of four children. Our family settled in Vancouver in a beautifully diverse neighbourhood. I was eighteen and still in high school when I got married. My husband was also from India and age nineteen. It was not an "arranged" marriage, however, at that age I did not have much of a voice. I lived a very sheltered life and was afraid of standing up for myself, so when the subject of marriage was brought up, I felt I had no option but to say yes. That being said, my husband and I ended up creating a good life for ourselves and our three children.

In 2012 we had been happily married for twenty-four years. At that time, I was working as a financial advisor with a large Canadian bank. We were the average middle-class working family living in the Lower Mainland. This was the year that my marriage would end, and I had to come to grips with what I had never seen coming. The ending of the marriage came as a shock not only to me but also to our families and friends. It was a sad time filled with much heartache and pain. It was a time in my life that I could not live one day at a time but only one breath at a time. I felt devastated by betrayal and hurt, for I never foresaw the end of my marriage. But end it did . . . and I had to pick up all the scattered pieces of my life.

> *I was so was very blessed to meet many healers, who introduced me to energy work and the incredible power of meditation. This was vital to my well-being . . .*

During this turbulent time, I needed support and guidance. I sought inner healing because I needed to stay strong. I was so was very blessed to meet many healers, who introduced me to energy work and the incredible power of meditation. This was vital to my well-being, and I never knew how much of a positive impact this was going to have in my life moving forward. Energy work helped me to stay strong and focused on what I needed to do. Without this healing, I am not sure how I would have coped. Meditation helped me to stay grounded and centred at a time of chaos and confusion.

That year I met Christa Faye Burka, my meditation teacher, who would also become a very dear friend. I think of her as my "soul mother." I started meditating with Christa's meditation group every Monday night. This weekly routine, combined with regular energy clearing sessions, became the foundation of my personal healing. Committing to the journey of healing my trauma allowed me to navigate this time with grace and compassion for myself and others around me.

When trauma enters your life, be it physical, emotional, or mental, you can find it very difficult to navigate daily routines. Both meditation and energy healing gave me the strength and peace to minimize the disfunction and chaos of the ending of a marriage and transform our family with as much grace as possible. So every Monday night I showed up at Christa's home and poured out my heart and my grief. Christa always held space for me to be heard; she honoured my feelings but never let me lose hope. We would meditate, become centred, and then have tea.

Christa passed away in 2022 and I will forever miss her. She was my spiritual guru and I loved her deeply. It is almost impossible to see the end of the tunnel when you are surrounded in such darkness, but Christa taught me that with work and dedication to your healing journey, the light will eventually come. The light will indeed embrace you and you will transform, to become the light for others.

Making self-care a priority

In South Asian culture, separation and divorce are very much frowned upon. As times have changed, however, marriage breakdown is becoming more common. The generation of women before me had minimal means to be independent and to provide for themselves. Thus, living in an unhappy marriage was the only option for many women. Not to say that separation and/ or divorce is always the right path. The path is yours alone. There is no right or wrong way in life, as the journey is a mystery and no one knows why or how people may come and go in your life.

> *This life is not meant to be lived for our culture, our society, or others. It is a gift we have all been given, and it is up to each of us individually to create the life that we cherish and honour.*

During the time when my marriage was ending, I cared little about cultural and social norms. I knew there was plenty of "noise" regarding our family situation, however, my priority was my mental health and my healing. I knew that in order to be a good mother, I needed to remain strong and take care of myself. Many people think that being selfless is taking care of everyone else, but I have always understood that you can only be selfless if you look after yourself first. Otherwise, you may find yourself becoming resentful of those you love the most. To sacrifice your needs for others can lead you to a very sad and depressing state. To truly honour yourself and your loved ones, you must prioritize yourself. There is nothing selfish about that.

I had a deep revelation that I would share with my daughters that year: that this life we have been gifted by our Creator was gifted to us individually. This life is not meant to be lived for our culture, our society, or others. It is a gift we have all been given, and it is up to each of us individually to create the life that we cherish and honour.

As the devastating events of 2012 unfolded, I found myself at times hanging on by just a thread. It came to a point in the fall that I could not remain in our marital home. After a very stressful week, I woke up one morning and literally heard the voice of God telling me, "You cannot stay under this roof for one more night." The message was so loud and powerful that I could not ignore it. I proceeded to call my dad and ask him if I could stay with him and my mother. I'll never forget his unwavering support. He told me to pack my stuff and he would pick me up in an hour. Barely holding on, I packed a suitcase and walked away from twenty-four years of marriage. It was one of the hardest days of my life. To this day, I have regret about the pain I caused my children by walking away without speaking with them first. Unfortunately, I was so emotionally depleted, I could not think clearly. Later my daughters joined me, whereas our son stayed with his father.

Relationships in transition

My daughters and I remained with my parents for a few months. It was a very challenging time and also a time to heal with my parents beside me. I now look back on and cherish those months, for my dear, beloved mom passed away in 2024. It was a time for me to heal, to regain clarity and strength, and to start over. With the support of my energy healing and my commitment to meditation and self-care, I remained grounded and centred as my ex and I proceeded to finalize our separation. I completed the separation agreement myself. We were able to resolve and separate our finances without the added cost of lawyers. This time went by like a blur and before we knew it, we were legally separated and living separate lives. How life can change in a heartbeat.

Throughout it all, I knew that it was of utmost importance to maintain a peaceful relationship with my ex. After all, he was the father of my children and we did have many good years together. I had met a very special energy healer, Cassandra, who I still refer to as my "love guru." She had a very gentle way of helping me navigate this journey. She gave me the best advice, which to this day I share with many others. She said to do my best to transition my relationship with my ex from that of husband and wife to that of friends. She said this would save me and my family a lot of heartache.

Shifting a relationship is a hard thing to do when you are in so much pain. However, I knew that I had to take into consideration what my entire family was going through and try my best to keep the drama to a minimum. It is very easy to fall into the "blame game" and things can spiral downward fast from there. This is not healthy for our mind and our spirit.

Regardless of the actions of one or both parties, in a breakup there is pain on both sides. My priority was always healing for my children. They were the innocent bystanders in the fallout of the divorce. At the very least I wanted to give them some semblance of peace during this chaotic time.

Since the separation, my ex and I have maintained a relatively peaceful relationship and we now have four grandchildren. We participate in family celebrations and show each other respect and consideration. This helps everyone heal and move forward in life. Being stuck in the past will always lead to more heartache and pain. It is important to forgive others, with the understanding that every ending will bring forth a new beginning.

It was during my divorce that I started to write poetry again. I had started writing in my preteen years and found it healing and therapeutic. In 2014 I became part of the writing group Royal City Poets and I was delighted to became a published poet. That was the start of a new, exciting journey. Now, many years later, I have had my poetry published in numerous anthologies worldwide. My own book of poetry *True Grace* was released in 2017, a collaboration with the amazing therapeutic watercolour artist Rita Koivunen. This publication is a poetry and art creation that comes from our heart and soul and aims to help others heal. Here is the title poem from that collection.

TRUE GRACE

When all deeds are forgiven
For every saint and sinner
When God showers his praise
This is true grace

When hurtful words fall on deaf ears
Your pain in my eyes is mirrored
When all but love is erased
This is true grace

When glares are replaced by a smile
When for a stranger you'd walk a mile
With affection every thought is laced
This is true grace

When we take the other's hand
Woman, child or man
And from anguish as one we brace
This is true grace

When there is no longer I or Me
When life belongs to Us and We
After the horrors some have faced
This is true grace

When the doors of hell have opened
But heaven has already spoken
We can see it on every face
This is true grace

A new creative direction

In 2014 my writing evolved into writing song lyrics. I had never studied music, so I was surprised by this. In 2017 my first song collaboration, "Preach," was recorded and released by the Canadian artist Michelle Joly. It is a pop song about self-empowerment. Since then, I have worked with other singers and songwriters to create new music.

As I continued to walk through doors, other doors would open. In 2021 the indie feature film *Roads of Ithriyah* was released by director Javier Badillo. I was the executive producer and my song "Roads" played during the film credits. My niece Simmi Lally recorded this song with recording artist Kalvonix. It was an amazing feeling to first have my words put to music and then hear the song in a movie.

I am currently working on more music, poetry, and film. I am excited to continue to share my words through poetry and lyrics. I have made peace with the past and have an understanding of change being an important aspect of our personal growth. As we grow and evolve in life, many people, places, and things will be given to us and taken away. It is important to have the ability to flow in the receiving and the letting go.

At the end of our time here, what will be remembered? Forgotten? Forgiven? Think about the ending as you go through the process of letting go, and create the environment you know that you and your family will thrive in. Stay strong throughout your journey and be at peace with your choices and your life. Nurture yourself and evolve into the You that you have built, stronger and wiser than ever before. Honour the journey that took you on this path of growth, healing, and living fully in your glory.

JAZ GILL

Jaz is an award-winning writer, poet, lyricist, and music and movie producer. She loves to collaborate with others to share creative talents.

In 2014 Jaz became a published poet, and since then she has been featured in numerous anthologies worldwide. In 2017 she published *True Grace*, her first poetry book, co-authored by artist Rita Koivunen. The same year her first song collaboration was released, the single "Preach" sung by Michelle Joly. Since then, Jaz has written lyrics for various music genres. In 2021 she became executive producer for the indie film *Roads of Ithriya*, beginning her journey of supporting filmmakers. Her lyrics are featured in music for *Roads of Ithriyah* and another film, *Dil Rakh: Gloves of Kin* (2023), and she is excited to continue her collaborations in music and film.

Jaz is a mother of three and a devoted grandmother who enjoys travelling and spending time with her family and friends.

🌐 jazgill.com

THE COURAGE TO CHANGE
BY SHANNON LITTLE

In life, change is the one thing that is constant. If we aren't flexible, adaptable, and willing to grow and learn from the changes that will inevitably face us throughout our life, we will become stagnant, break, or remain stuck on hold.

I HAVE ALWAYS BEEN a happy, positive, high-energy, look-for-the-good kind of person. I love challenges, and not only would I complete any challenge put before me, I would do so to the absolute best of my abilities. My drive, spirit, energy, and perfectionist nature have served me well throughout my life, as I accomplished every goal and dream I pursued.

After graduating with honours in 2000, with two degrees from the University of British Columbia, I began my high-school teaching career that same year. Teaching was everything I imagined it would be. I was home. I loved my students and my colleagues. All of my classes provided me with daily ongoing challenges and new experiences, and because of my passion and love for sports and music, I was able to give back through coaching and organizing rock concerts as fundraisers for school field trips.

My life was full. People called me the "Energizer Bunny." But intuitively I knew my health was failing. After five years of the wrong medical tests and two misdiagnoses by specialists, my life was forever altered in July 2003 when I was diagnosed with Cushing's syndrome, a rare hormonal disorder also called hypercortisolism, and a benign brain tumour on my pituitary gland. (It was discovered later, after countless MRIs, that I had two benign brain tumours on my pituitary gland.)

I continued to work that next fall semester and kept up an active social life, but the pain, anxiety, fear, and countless number of doctor's appointments I was having to attend and medical tests I was having to take became overwhelming. I was literally spiralling downward and my monkey brain would not let me sleep. The doctors and pharmacists were trying every medication (except narcotics and botox) to ease my varying symptoms. I felt like a walking pharmacy.

At this early stage of my diagnosis, my family and I did not know if I was going to live or die. I had just celebrated my thirtieth birthday. Twenty years ago there wasn't a lot of information about Cushing's, with only ten per every one million people being diagnosed with it, and today the syndrome is still quite rare.

After much research and many medical appointments, my parents and I accepted that the transsphenoidal hypophysectomy surgery to remove the tumour was a risk, but would ideally cure me of Cushing's and let me continue living life as I knew it. So on December 4, 2003, at 9:30 a.m., the three of us met with my neurosurgeon at Vancouver General Hospital (VGH) to discuss my upcoming surgery. The surgeon explained that my case was extremely high-risk, with a success rate of only 30 percent, and a greater chance of me having a stroke or bleeding out on the table during the procedure.

I was now to become a patient at the BC Cancer Agency and begin receiving radiation treatment. As my surgeon talked of this new plan, I vividly recall the out-of-body experience of seeing myself and my parents sitting across from the surgeon as we looked at my MRI brain scan on his computer in his crowded little office at VGH. How could I possibly be a patient at the cancer agency? I didn't have cancer. My tumour was benign. There was such a disconnect between all the emotions I was experiencing. I felt relief at not having to have brain surgery, but I did not fully comprehend why I was going to become a cancer agency patient when my tumour was benign. As I had been doing for months, in order to survive and keep going, I compartmentalized this latest information so I could process it another time.

Later that same day, I attended a celebration of life for a friend I knew from high school. He had died tragically, in a car accident, at the age of thirty. Reuniting with old friends, and with one special friend from my past whom I hadn't seen in years, was good for my soul, and reminded me more than ever just how important and precious life is.

In January 2004, I started to teach the spring semester, but by the third week I was on short-term medical leave, as I began prepping for treatment at the cancer agency. I started receiving five weeks of radiation treatment on my brain tumour on February 6, 2004, and was classified as a teacher on long-term medical disability.

The cancer agency may represent or mean many things to people, depending on how it has affected them or their families personally. To me, it was my saving grace. I found comfort and security when I walked through the doors of the agency, and I will forever be grateful for the treatment and care I received there. As a patient I benefited from the art therapy program, the relaxation therapy program, meditation courses, counselling, pain clinics, and, of course, care from the medical team and radiation treatments. I continued to attend the relaxation therapy sessions for years after my radiation treatment ended, particularly when I was struggling and in need of support from a group who would understand what I was dealing with, without judgment.

Over the next couple of years as I began my healing journey, I dipped my toe into the world of volunteering. I started with Pacific Assistance Dogs Society (PADS) and was a puppy

Everyone always knew me to be so strong, to always have a smile on my face, no matter what I was going through. I had become an expert at disguising my pain.

cuddler. I absolutely loved this as I was unable to own a puppy but could benefit from all the cuddles these adorable pups needed and honestly I did too. I also wrote for an online newspaper and took a night-school writing course. The loss of my grandma in 2006 profoundly affected me. However, it was just another loss that I compartmentalized to process at a later time.

I went back to teach one class from 2007 to 2008. However, sadly this proved to be too taxing for my health, and I officially went on long-term medical leave in June 2008. As all of my closest friends and family members were getting engaged, married, and starting families during these years, I realized that my life was taking a completely different path. Getting married and having children had never been a top priority for me, but I noticed that although I never lost my lifetime friends, we saw each other less often, and I was beginning to seek out new friends and acquaintances.

On January 8, 2009, my parents and I met with a board of ten doctors led by two of the top neurosurgeons in Vancouver (one being my original surgeon) to review my case again. We learned that surgery for a Cushing's tumour had to be all-or-nothing. Because of the aggressive nature of these tumours, despite being benign, if any segment is left behind after removal, the patient will still have active Cushing's syndrome. My tumours are wrapped around my carotid arteries, which are uniquely S-shaped in my brain, which makes it impossible for the tumours to be removed. We were also informed that any benefits from the radiation treatment might not take effect until ten years post treatment.

Once again, I felt my life was put on hold. I knew I would always have Cushing's. At the same time, I would never be a candidate for surgery due to my anatomy. And although part of me felt relieved, as an extremely high-risk brain surgery never did sound appealing, I was mentally, physically, emotionally, and spiritually exhausted.

Finding community through volunteering

Everyone always knew me to be so strong, to always have a smile on my face, no matter what I was going through. I had become an expert at disguising my pain. On the outside I look like the picture of health. This has been both a blessing and a curse. I was grateful I didn't "look sick." But it caused me great anxiety if I felt the need to explain, particularly to new people in my life, why I wasn't working, or why I needed to rest after only being awake for a few hours.

Just after the 2010 Winter Olympics in Vancouver, I struggled with severe thoughts of suicide and not wanting to be here. No one knew. I felt so alone. Intuitively I knew I wasn't alone. I had and have always had a huge support system. But as anyone who has struggled with depression and anxiety knows, the demons are dark and overpowering. And they will convince you no one cares, and that you are all alone. I fought through the darkness, and what kept me here is my belief that I had more to do with my life and I couldn't hurt my parents.

Volunteering became my next "calling." I turned it into a career of sorts, since I was unable to return to work or any regular paid employment. My love for music was fulfilled when I volunteered with an entertainment company as a music scout around the city and as an emcee at a local jazz club. I made lifetime friends and was able to enjoy dressing up and discovering new bands and entertainment. In 2011 and 2012, respectively, I began volunteering with BC Children's Hospital, teaching in their school room and writing for their online magazine, as well as volunteering for Ronald McDonald House Charities. Through the latter and writing and doing interviews for an online magazine, I eventually met a whole new crowd of friends, connections, and even some new loves, which led to more opportunities and adventures around my city and the world.

I began volunteering with Lions Gate Hospital Foundation in 2016 as both of my parents had gone through serious health issues and gratefully survived, due to the wonderful care and treatment they received from their doctors and nurses at Lions Gate.

Through my passion for writing I connected with some people who asked if I would be interested in volunteering in the making of a short film at the Dunbar Theatre. This project turned colleagues into friends, and a few years later we made another film at the Dunbar and even submitted it to film festivals.

I have always walked to the beat of my own drum, making my own way, following my heart, knowing that what is truly meant for me will never pass me by.

Most recently I have begun volunteering as a stylist with the amazing organization Dress for Success Vancouver. I absolutely love how this charity helps women find beautiful outfits and accessories that light them up so they can feel their best as they go out into the world for job interviews, into their new place of employment, to school, to special occasions, or perhaps to start a new life in Canada. Everyone who works and volunteers at Dress for Success is so wonderful, and I feel so grateful to be a part of this organization.

I have never stopped learning and continually strive to keep my mind active through taking webinars, reading books that interest me, learning new languages, and travelling. One of my greatest dreams was achieved in 2021, when I self-published, with the help of one of my lifetime friends, my own book on Amazon. It contains original quotes, poetry, and prose accompanied by my own black-and-white photography. I followed it up with my second book in June 2024.

Giving back provides perspective

Over the years my volunteering with these organizations eventually slowed and some completely stopped. I found different interests and passions. But as always, my health would dictate what I could or could not do. This was and still is extremely frustrating for me, but after twenty years of dealing with my health, I have learned many coping strategies and skills, such as mindfulness meditation, to manage my feelings of loss, frustration, anger, hopelessness, and sadness, and to always look at all the benefits and good that happened because of my situation.

That being said, it doesn't mean I don't grieve the losses that meant so much to me. I had been an athlete when I was young, excelling in all the sports I played and being particularly drawn to physically aggressive activities and sports like karate, volleyball, and snowboarding. They allowed me to release my energy that was always in excess. However, after being diagnosed with Cushing's I was also diagnosed with fibromyalgia. This, along with some of my other conditions, stops me from participating in most of the physical activities I would love to partake in. So I now enjoy practising yoga, walking, hiking, playing golf, and dancing.

In life, change is the one thing that is constant. If we aren't flexible, adaptable, and willing to grow and learn from the changes that will inevitably face us throughout our life, we will become stagnant, break, or remain stuck on hold. "Change is good." These three simple words have resonated with me over the past fourteen years after a dear friend said them to me when I was struggling so greatly with my losses. Confronting, challenging, and ultimately changing our assumptions and attitudes—about ourselves, about others in society—takes courage but brings great gains.

I have always walked to the beat of my own drum, making my own way, following my heart, knowing that what is truly meant for me will never pass me by. I don't believe in regrets and believe we learn from life lessons. I am not a saint, and for those who have called me a "Little angel," I always joke that my halo hangs crooked off my devil horns.

My childhood was idyllic, and for that I am truly blessed and grateful. My youth and twenties were years that I absolutely loved and would relive in a heartbeat. After being diagnosed before I turned thirty with a rare disease, and eventually two inoperable brain tumours, I lost my career as a teacher and my identity, which had a profound effect on my social life. This was definitely not the future I had planned for myself. But I still never gave up. I kept persevering, intuitively knowing my purpose in life was not yet fulfilled.

During my forties, by following my passions through volunteering, I finally felt like I was beginning to live again. Now, as I enter my fifties, I reflect back on all the people I have met and the life experiences I have had to date because of my health journey, and I feel gratitude in my heart and believe the best years are still to come.

Some of the most important things I have learned over the last twenty years of dealing with my personal health issues and volunteering are that when you give back to others, whether or not they are in greater need, you are no longer focused on your own situation. Giving back may not alleviate your problems or your pain, and it certainly does not make your situation less valid or important, but it does help put things into perspective. It reminds you not to sweat the *little* things. To take pause and enjoy every moment of life. To be kind and live with compassion and grace for yourself, for those you love, and for everyone you meet, because you never know what people are dealing with. I try never to judge a book by its cover. And to always look for the good, in every situation.

SHANNON LITTLE

Shannon holds degrees in human kinetics and education from the University of British Columbia and began her career as a high-school teacher. Her fondest memories in her teaching career include being witness to young minds becoming critical thinkers, creating a school magazine, and taking students on field trips into Vancouver and across Canada.

Writing has always been one of Shannon's greatest passions and outlets for her to express her feelings. In 2021 she self-published on Amazon her first book, *"Little" Musings on Life and Everything In Between*, a collection of her original quotes, poetry, prose, and black-and-white photography. She followed this book in June 2024 with *MORE "Little" Musings on Life and Everything In Between*.

Shannon makes her home in Vancouver, BC. She enjoys spending time with her loved ones, listening to music, staying physically active, travelling, continually learning, networking, and connecting, and she believes in always looking for the good.

🌐 littellewritings.com

ⓕ Shannon.Little.8

GIVE YOURSELF PERMISSION
BY GINA BEST

You don't need to fit into anyone else's mould. You don't need to live up to society's expectations. The only person you need permission from is yourself.

WHILE HAVING LUNCH with a good friend, I told her about the chapter I was writing for this book, with the theme of defying social expectations. She looked at me with a big grin, laughed, and said, "That's so you!"

Her comment hit me. It was casual but deeply true. I've spent most of my life going against the grain, breaking through societal norms—sometimes consciously, other times without even realizing it. That one remark triggered a flood of thoughts and memories. I started thinking: *How do I narrow them down to just one story for this chapter?*

The thing is, it's not easy to pick just one moment. In so many ways, my entire life has been about challenging what others thought I should be. But if I'm being real with you, for many years, I was fighting an internal battle. I did what I thought others expected of me, but in my own way, I was always pushing against the edges. It wasn't until about twelve years ago that I really began to understand this.

I was walking around with these "rules" in my head—rules I had picked up along the way, rules I thought I had to follow. They were unwritten, but they had a huge influence on me. They shaped how I behaved, how I moved through my life, how I related to others. But when I finally started to examine those rules, I realized something: most of them were total bullshit. They weren't my rules at all. They were rules I had made up, rules that had been imposed on me by society, by family, by expectations. And guess what? They didn't serve me.

> *Judgment is inevitable. The world is full of opinions, and they'll come at you from every direction—about how you look, how you act, how you live your life.*

When I finally started doing the personal work—really digging deep into those rules and questioning them—I felt a huge sense of freedom. I let go of the rules that didn't serve me, and I started writing my own. That's when everything changed. I stopped living my life according to what I thought I *should* do and started living on my terms.

So now I'm wondering: *What story will have the most impact?* What story will show those following in my footsteps that it's okay to be unapologetically themselves, without hesitation, no matter what society, social media, or their own self-doubt tells them?

In the end, this chapter is more than just my story of defying expectations. It's about giving others permission to do the same. Because here's what I know for sure: living up to other people's expectations is a trap. It keeps you from being your authentic self. It keeps you from being free. So the real question is: How do we break free from that?

Judgment: The loudest voice has to be yours

When my nineteen-year-old son told me they worry about what others think, their words hurt my heart. I saw so much of myself in them—worried about being judged, about saying the "wrong" thing or being the "wrong" person. I know that feeling intimately. But here's the truth I've learned over the years: judgment is inevitable. The world is full of opinions, and they'll come at you from every direction—about how you look, how you act, how you live your life. You can't avoid them. But how much of that judgment do you allow to shape you?

I told my kid, "Look, you've got green hair. People are going to judge. That's not something you can stop. What matters is that your voice—the way *you* feel about yourself—is the loudest one you hear."

It took me years to learn that. Even now, I have to remind myself. But the truth is, people will judge you no matter what. They'll judge your clothes, your words, your choices, your lifestyle. They'll judge you for things that don't even matter. But you don't have to care. *You* get to decide what matters. You get to decide how boldly you show up in the world. That is your power.

Embracing my story: Every scar, every tattoo

This brings me to my own journey. As I said, I've spent years feeling the pressure to conform, to fit in, to be what others thought I should be. Especially as a woman, body image is a battlefield. We're conditioned from such a young age to believe our value is tied to how we look. How much time have I wasted fighting with myself over this, hating my body, wishing it looked different—skinnier, prettier, more like the version society told me I needed to be?

It took me a long time to make peace with my body. And even now, it's a daily practice. That insecure sixteen-year-old version of me still tries to surface, especially when it comes to things like dating. I've learned to silence her, to remind her that I'm not that girl anymore—I'm stronger, wiser, and worth so much more than those old insecurities. When I look in the mirror today, I don't see that insecure girl. I see the life I've lived—every scar, every tattoo, every line tells a part of my story. My body holds those stories. Some are written in ink; others are etched into me through experience. And for me, many of my stories are visible, and I'm proud of that.

There's a bit of a tattoo on my neck, but my eyes always fall down to the full tattoo that covers my left breast. It's the one that gives me pause. The phoenix, rising from the flames—a symbol of rebirth and transformation—covers the scars left behind from my battle with breast cancer. My left breast is an implant, something I had to fight for after a partial mastectomy. Beneath that phoenix are the scars from five surgeries. Every time I look at the phoenix, I'm reminded of those years—dealing not only with cancer, but with the medical system, with my doubts, with the fear that tried to crush me.

But here's the thing: I made it through. That tattoo isn't just decoration. It's a declaration. Breast cancer doesn't define me, and it never will. When I see that phoenix, I don't just see a piece of art—I see my journey, my story. There's a bittersweet beauty in that ink. It's a reminder that I'm not the same person I was before those surgeries. I'm stronger now. I'm more resilient. The phoenix rises from the ashes again and again, just like I do. Each day is a new beginning, and I'm still standing.

Then there's my left arm, where my first big tattoo sits. It tells the story of my family, of where I come from and who I am. Cherry blossoms stretch across my skin, a nod to Vancouver, where I now live. Beneath the trees, roots stretch down into the water, a nod to where I come from, my connection to both coasts. Four fish swim in that water—one for me, one for each of my boys, and one for my ex-husband, who remains a good friend and co-parent.

This tattoo is my map. It's my reminder of where I've been, the family I've built, the love I've experienced, and the journey we're all on. The fish swim freely, just as we do—navigating our own paths through life, but always tied together by the invisible thread of family.

On my right arm, there's another tattoo—bold and bright. It's one of my favourites. I call it "From Grief I Grow." It's a vibrant skull with a butterfly—a reminder that grief doesn't break us; it changes us. This tattoo conveys the message and reminds me grief doesn't have to stop us in our tracks. It changes us and allows us to grow.

Grief never really goes away, does it? It sticks around, lingers, shifts. But we grow around it. That's what this tattoo means to me. The butterfly rises from the skull—fragile but resilient—symbolizing how even after loss, beauty can emerge. It takes time, sure, and the journey sucks. This ink reminds me that despite the grief I've carried, I've gained perspective, strength, and the wisdom that comes from loss.

Farther down my right arm is another tattoo—smaller, but just as heavy. It's for my brother, whom I lost too soon, and for the twin babies I never got to hold. It simply says, "At What Cost?" That's a question I carry with me every single day. It's a reminder that there's a price to everything, especially when it comes to the ways we give of ourselves.

> When I look at my body now, I see the full picture. I see the journey I've been on, and it's written across my skin in tattoos and scars.

For years I was the yes person. I gave and gave and gave, without ever thinking about what all of the giving was taking from me. Now I stop and ask myself: *At what cost?* Is this worth my energy, my time, my peace? This question has become my compass. It's what keeps me grounded, what keeps me from running on empty. I no longer sacrifice myself for the sake of others. I've learned that my time, my energy, and my peace are valuable—and it's okay to protect them.

Tattoos, for me, are so much more than just ink on skin. They are my story, my experiences, my growth, and, most importantly, my resilience. The phoenix on my breast isn't just a beautiful design—it's a testament to my strength. It's a reminder that I fought through surgeries and fear and came out on the other side stronger than I ever.

When I look at my body now, I see the full picture. I see the journey I've been on, and it's written across my skin in tattoos and scars. I've battled with my body for years—wishing it was different, wishing it looked more like what society told me it should. I fought that internal war for so long. My belly, especially, was always a source of frustration. I wanted it to be flatter, tighter, more like those impossible bodies on magazine covers.

But now? Now, I look at my belly, and I see the part of me that nourishes me. It's soft, yes, but it's strong. It's part of my body, and my body has carried me through this life with strength and endurance. I don't hate my belly anymore. I thank it. It doesn't need to look like anything other than what it is. My body isn't here to conform to someone else's ideal. My body is here to support me, to help me live, to be a vessel for all my experiences.

And then there's the scar on my left leg—a six-inch reminder of the camping accident I had with my boys. That accident landed me in the hospital, sent me into emergency surgery, and kept me in a brace from hip to ankle for months. The recovery sucked, both physically and mentally. That scar? It's another mark of resilience. Even now, the leg acts up sometimes, reminding me of that accident. But every time I look at that scar, I feel proud. I got through that. I healed. I came out the other side. That scar reminds me of what my body is capable of.

Professional success: Breaking moulds in business

It's not just in my personal life where I've defied expectations. My professional life has been just as much about breaking moulds. I've spent over twenty years building my own business from the ground up. I've stood on stages across North America, speaking to rooms full of people. But even after all that time, every time I walk into a new room, I can feel the stares.

People look at me—at my blue hair, my tattoos, my style—and they size me up. I see it in their eyes. They're thinking, *Who is this woman, and why is she here?* I don't fit into their preconceived notion of what a successful businesswoman should look like. Years ago, the judgment would have bothered me. I would have worn more "professional" clothes, covered up my tattoos, and tried to blend in.

But not anymore. Now I walk into those rooms fully as myself. I've earned the right to be there, and I don't need to conform to anyone else's idea of success. My blue hair, my tattoos, my style—they don't define my ability to do great work. *I* define that. I've learned that my authenticity is my power, and I'm not interested in changing myself to make others comfortable.

When people meet me, they usually have one of two reactions. Either they're confused because they can't reconcile the woman standing in front of them with the successful businesswoman they have heard about. Or they're relieved. Relieved because I'm not pretending. Relieved because they're finally seeing someone who isn't trying to fit into the mould. Either way, I keep showing up as myself, because that's the only way I know how to be. And it's worked for me.

For years, when people asked me how I was, I had a default answer: "I'm fine." It was the polite, socially acceptable thing to say, even when it wasn't true. Even when I was exhausted or overwhelmed or struggling, I'd smile and say I was fine because that's what people expected. I didn't want to make anyone uncomfortable by telling them the truth. But over the years, I've learned that pretending to be fine doesn't serve anyone, least of all myself.

Now when people ask how I am, I answer honestly. If I'm struggling, I say so. If I'm great, I say that too. I've stripped away the filter. I'm done with pretending to be fine for other people's comfort. I speak my truth, even if it's messy. Even if it's raw. Even if it's uncomfortable.

And here's what I want you to take away from all this: You don't need to fit into anyone else's mould. You don't need to live up to society's expectations. The only person you need permission from is yourself.

It took me a lot of years to understand that the rules I had been living by weren't mine. Years to finally give myself permission to live authentically. And I know how hard that can be. I know how easy it is to get trapped in the expectations of others, to shape yourself into something you're not just to make other people happy. But honestly, you will never be truly happy until you give yourself permission to be who you are, unapologetically, scars, tattoos, blue hair, and all.

It's easy to get caught up in trying to be everything for everyone else. But you can't. And you shouldn't. Living for other people will drain you dry, and it will leave you feeling hollow. It's not selfish to put yourself first. It's necessary. You have to give yourself permission to live fully as you are, without hesitation, without apology.

I've spent years fighting against expectations—expectations from society, from others, and even from myself. What I've learned through it all is that your power lies in your authenticity. It lies in your ability to strip away the crap, to let go of the rules that don't serve you, and to show up as yourself, fully and unapologetically.

I've learned to embrace my body, my scars, my tattoos, my blue hair, and my story—because they all tell the truth of who I am. And there's power in that truth. There's power in owning your story, in standing in your power, even when the world tries to tell you who you should be.

So give yourself permission to be who you are, completely. Let go of the fear of judgment. Let go of the pressure to conform. Live your life on your terms. Be true to yourself—scars, tattoos, blue hair, and all. That's where your power lies. In the end, it's your life. Live it in a way that makes you proud. Live it authentically, without hesitation. Because there is no one else like you, and the world needs you—the real you.

That's the truth I'm living. And I hope, for your sake, you'll start living it too.

GINA BEST

Gina is a serial entrepreneur and a maverick mentor with a penchant for pushing people's buttons and compelling business owners to deal with their personal obstacles so they can attack their businesses with passion and authenticity. Gina owns one of BC's largest mortgage brokerages, runs her own business-building workshops, mentors entrepreneurs, speaks to and inspires audiences across the continent, and still finds—rather, makes—time to be a mostly patient mom to two wild boys, a witty and wonderful friend, a shoe hoarder, and a bold and gracious mentor to young businesswomen in her community. Gina is the first to admit that she has it all and she earned it—through hard work, tears, anger, self-doubt, grit, and hustle.

🌐 gina.best
🌐 ginaknowsbest.com

THERE IS NO ALTERNATIVE
BY FIONA FORESTELL

In my mind, there is no alternative. If I shut off, shut down, become judge and jury, I have allowed the outside world to prevail. Staying loyal and true to my values, beliefs, and core principles is where I choose to reside.

HAVE YOU EVER HAD A DEFINING MOMENT in your life? That aha moment which changed the trajectory of your life forever? This is the story of such an event that happened in my life. It didn't reveal itself as an explosion of fireworks but rather like embers in a fire that was nearly burned out, yet there was just enough spark left for the fire to reignite.

Let me introduce myself. I was born in South Africa and moved to Scotland when I was twelve. After finishing my higher education, I worked as an au pair in Paris for a year and then lived in Wales before joining the British Army, serving Queen and Country for the following eight years. I left the military to start a family and was living, at the time, in a village in England.

Now that I have set the scene, you can see that I was well travelled and my accent was certainly a mix of different countries. Did I fit into society? Well, to be honest, I always did feel different (don't we all?) due to my background, my upbringing, and my previous job. Though in truth, feeling different didn't stop me from making friends, getting along with other people, and always being helpful.

I love to run, which you could say would put me in the minority. I had joined the Royal Corps of Signals, the army's communications unit, though while living in Germany, I trained to be a physical training instructor. Fitness comes naturally for me. As I mentioned at the start of my story, I was born in South

Africa and was raised running around in the hot sun with no shoes on my feet, which was what all the children did in those days. Some of you might remember the South African athlete Zola Budd running barefoot in the 1984 Olympic Games.

Fast-forward a couple of decades, and I would still be running though now in my runners (what I called "trainers"), dressed appropriately for the colder climate in the United Kingdom in nondescript leggings and well-worn sweat tops. I would run around the village with my white German shepherd, Shingi, before becoming pregnant with my eldest daughter, Katy. I even ran while

> *To be frank, serving alongside thirty male physical training instructors in a gymnasium at a basic training unit . . . was much easier and more straightforward than spending time with a group of women.*

pregnant alongside our dog up to three months before giving birth. Then I was running around the village with a dog and stroller before I became pregnant with my second daughter, Libby. And yes, you guessed right, I was running pregnant with a stroller and a dog until eventually pushing a stroller with my two babies and my dog.

Let's see, did I stand out from the crowd? Probably, though honestly I wasn't conscious of that at the time. I was just focused on staying fit and healthy. In addition, my dog needed and loved the exercise.

One day, after dropping off my eldest daughter at daycare, I was about to go for a run with my youngest daughter and my dog when one of the other moms asked me, "Are you really going running round the village looking like that?" I was taken aback by her question and replied, "You know I am going for a run and not walking in a fashion show."

Afterwards while on my run, I started to really think about what she had asked me, and to my surprise I realized that this was the one time every day (I would run five times a week) that I was actually in a "fashion show," as everyone could see me running around the village, and for the record, my look was not glamorous at all. I would usually have dirt on my runners and splashed mud up the back of my leggings, my hair would be tied back in a scruffy ponytail, and my face would be bright red as I was huffing and puffing, running up the hills. There would even sometimes be dried sweat on my top (I mean, who washes their running clothes every time they exercise?) and, of course, I would not smell good.

After giving my outfit some thought, I decided it was too late to change anything. I had already been running around the village for three years, and there was nothing I could do to change people's impressions. On the bright side, I was proud of myself for being committed to my health and fitness. I liked dedicating myself to achieving my goals and was proud of the discipline I had created in my life to show up for myself.

The invitation arrives

Shortly afterwards our family moved to the "posh" neighbourhood of the village, where the in-crowd lived. You know, the moms who drove Land Rovers to drop off and pick up their kids from school. No offence intended here: I would just like you to understand the importance for many in this neighbourhood (including me, by the way) to "fit in" through material possessions that held more value. Sure, these moms were all friendly enough, though I always felt some distance from them—and not because I did not drive a Land Rover.

Do you ever stop to wonder why you think the way you do? I have always been a "people pleaser," and the thought of someone not liking me would really upset me. Even though I am a natural extrovert and have an effervescent character, empathy is one of my top five strengths. While I am proud of this, I also know that your biggest strength can be your biggest weakness. I would always, always say yes to everyone and everything, which at times became detrimental to me.

Integrity is also a virtue I hold high in my convictions. "My word is my bond" is extremely important to me. I always say to my girls, "Mean what you say, say what you mean, and don't say what you don't mean." When we announce to people we are going to do something and don't follow through, our lack of integrity starts to chip away at our self-confidence, self-respect, and self-love.

To be frank, serving alongside thirty male physical training instructors in a gymnasium at a basic training unit and being the only female physical training instructor was much easier and more straightforward than spending time with a group of women. Men, more often than not, will say exactly how they feel, with no hidden agenda. Among the other moms around the school gates, no one actually said anything to me, though (as we all know) a woman's intuition is more powerful than anything. Even without applying any logic, the feeling that I did not belong was so deep inside, I needed no explanation. Have you ever heard the phrase "You know when you know"? It is exactly as the laws of the Universe dictate—the sun will always rise in the morning, the moon will always rise at night, and spring will always follow winter.

As I was pondering these feelings, I was also curious whether perhaps the delicate, emotional side of me, the Cancer water sign, was being overly sensitive. After all, most of the moms had known each other a lot longer than they had known me; they had also been born locally and raised in the same village. I was a newcomer, so being accepted into their group was going to take time.

And boy, oh boy, did it take time. A very long time. Six months went by, then one year, two years, and finally three years later, I was invited to a jewellery party that one of the moms was hosting at her house. Feeling excited is an understatement. I was ecstatic! Finally, this was my chance to make friends, and I am not just referring to friends who talk about the weather. I am talking about friends who really care for one another. You know, those friends you can have a heart-to-heart discussion with and know that whatever you share, it will go no further. The bosom friend you can call a "soul sister," since you both have the utmost respect and love for one another.

Of course, if I had to choose a friend like this from the animal kingdom, it would be a dog. Not only are they the most loyal animals in the world, no matter how your day has gone, good or bad, or how you are feeling, their love for you is always unconditional. That's the type of friend I was hoping to have. A friend who wants the sum of the whole, not just a small piece of me.

So, this was my big chance, my breakthrough at last. An added factor to raise my vibration was that I was having a night out with "the girls." As all the moms out there know, when you have young children, going out is a rare occurrence, and even though it was a house party it felt like a night on the town!

> *All these years I had spent making such a huge effort—all the energy, goodwill, kindness, everything I had done—amounted to nothing because they had already made up their minds.*

The night of the party arrived and I turned up at the house, on time, with a bottle of wine in my hand. I had even made the effort to find out the hostess's favourite type of wine, as I was keen to make a good impression. Most of the moms in the room I had met before except for one. She had just moved into our estate one month before. She seemed lovely and had moved from London, so I felt she was open-minded. We chatted for a while until I had an overwhelming feeling to ask her a question. To this day, I am still not sure where the question came from. (Perhaps it had been brewing inside of me for many years.) Also, I was surprised at how brave I was to ask a relative stranger, though I did it anyway.

I asked her how she had come to be invited to the party. I mentioned the fact that I had already been living in the estate for three years and had waited a long time for an invitation, yet here she was, only one month after arriving, with an invitation. Her answer to my question was that defining moment in my life that changed everything, and I was never the same person ever again. My self-image, my "map of the world," my perception—everything changed forever in that moment.

Her answer to my question was this. "How tall are you? Five foot seven? You have long blonde hair and are tall and lean. I have seen you run around the village with your dog." In a dazed and confused state, I replied, "But what has that got to do with having to wait so long to be accepted?" She went on to say, "Take a look at me. I am five foot two, short brown hair, and two stone overweight." Still none the wiser, I said to her, "I still don't understand." To which she replied in a short, concise comment: "They are jealous of you!"

What? I could not believe it. *What does she mean they are jealous of me?* I mean, why would they be jealous of me? "But I'm a really nice person," I said. Again she directly pointed out to me that it didn't matter how nice a person I was. It was obvious to her that the other moms were jealous of me and still were. Tonight was a token gesture and that was the reason I had been invited.

A valuable life lesson

It felt as if I had been struck by a bolt of lightning. All these years I had spent making such a huge effort—all the energy, goodwill, kindness, everything I had done—amounted to nothing because they had already made up their minds. The newcomer was right, and as I sit here and write this to you, I am so grateful for the seed that was planted from the harsh lesson I was taught that day. A seed only grows in the dark towards the light. The beginning of the day doesn't start when the sun rises, it starts in the middle of the night, in darkness, when the clock strikes.

Without that valuable lesson in life, I would never have become a successful entrepreneur with 4,500 people in my organization, spanning six countries. The lesson I learned is that there is nothing you can do to make people like you, nothing in this world. The decision-making process is "on them." Letting go of what others thought of me was the best thing I ever did. When you attempt to control, you contract; when you release, you expand.

All I can do is to show up as the best version of myself. The person who is always giving, caring, sharing, no matter what other people think of me. That is none of my concern. By setting yourself free of these thoughts, you will start to attract your tribe, the right people who resonate with you.

This life lesson echoed the story of my beautiful dog at the time, Shingi. I had him with me while running with the recruits in the army as well as running around the village with my girls for all those years. One afternoon, out of nowhere, another dog bit Shingi when he was only a sweet, naive young puppy. I was so afraid that this attack would change his temperament.

You see, in life, so many people allow the outer world to influence their inner world. We are always in control of how we respond or react to others. Even though we aren't able to control their actions, we are always in charge of how we respond. That is our choice. If we change our nature to suit others, we have handed over our power. I was nervous that after being bitten Shingi's temperament would change, but thankfully it never did.

I teach people: when you get a difficult message on your phone, do not answer it for 24 hours. This keeps you in control of your response and allows you to respond rather than react, which would lower your vibration to match the person sending you the message. In 24 hours, either the problem will have been resolved, the person will have come to their senses and apologized, or at the least they will have found a solution by themselves.

My mom always tells me that I am a "welcome doormat," allowing lots of people to rub dirt on my face. She is right, I *am* a "welcome doormat" (a much wiser person now). This is how I choose to live my life still to this day, choosing being kind over being right and being open to everything and attached to nothing. In my mind, there is no alternative. If I shut off, shut down, become judge and jury, I have allowed the outside world to prevail. Staying loyal and true to my values, beliefs, and core principles is where I choose to reside.

All life lessons are opportunities to learn and grow beyond adversity. Due to that valuable life lesson, I stopped attempting to "fit in" and be accepted. I found my own divine inner strength and power and stood up for what I believed in, which set me on a glorious path of becoming an entrepreneur and being able to influence and inspire thousands of people. I hope from reading about my life lesson that you too will start to love yourself unconditionally, for that is when the true magic starts to happen. When you wake up your inner voice of beauty, your passion will take over, enabling you to become the person you were truly meant to be. Just as every snowflake is different and has its own unique design, so too do you.

FIONA FORESTELL

Fiona was born and raised in South Africa. After her family moved back to Scotland, she continued her higher education there before travelling the world. She joined the British Army in 1992, serving in the Royal Corps of Signals and specializing as a physical training instructor. She left the military to start a family in 2007 and at the same time joined a network marketing firm, building her business as an independent consultant to achieve the highest levels in the company.

Fiona has achieved multiple awards in her career, having been an entrepreneur for almost eighteen years. She has spoken all over the world, including in front of 14,000 people in Las Vegas at her company event in 2011. Last year she spoke in Arizona, Liverpool, and on multiple Zoom calls in front of thousands of people. Fiona is passionate about connecting like-minded women and empowering them to be more so that they can have more.

🌐 fionaforestell.arbonne.com
in fiona-forestell-2355781
f fiona.mccarthy.94

ABOUT CATHY KUZEL

This is one connected woman! A dynamic speaker, professional mentor, and business expert with a deep knowledge of the art of human connections, Cathy Kuzel has been networking and building successful business relationships for more than forty years and is increasingly sought after as an expert on all things "small biz."

Recognized as one of the Top Ten Mentors in Canada by Startup Canada and a YWCA Women of Distinction Awards finalist, Cathy finds great personal fulfillment in helping others succeed. She combines her intuitive understanding and strong technical background in the theory of business with phenomenal energy and imaginative ways to get even the most skeptical fired up to explore the value of "connecting."

Beyond creating and chairing The Connected Woman Association, Cathy's passion for and dedication to helping women entrepreneurs succeed extends to her involvement with WeBC, Futurpreneur, Junior Achievement, her community, and the Connected Woman's micro-loan initiative through Kiva (to name just a few).

Cathy also knows that "Every Woman has a Story. Every Woman has a Voice. Every Woman deserves to be Heard," so she has created an amazing opportunity to share women's stories through podcasts and her book series *When Women Talk*. Her purpose is to help you Stand Up, Stand Out, and Step Forward. In her own words, "I am a firm believer in 'Knowledge shared is success magnified.' "

For more information on courses and keynotes by Cathy, visit her website cathykuzel.com or call the office directly at +1 (604) 980-5585.

- CathyKuzel.com
- WhenWomenTalk.ca
- cathykuzeltcw
- TheConnectedWoman

TWO POWERFUL ANTHOLOGIES

"A remarkable book that inspires, uplifts, and challenges you through the personal stories of ten women who are entrepreneurs, businesswomen, mothers, counsellors, and so much more. Their stories will make you sit up and want to celebrate their achievements!"

To order additional copies of books in the *When Women Talk* series, visit whenwomentalk.ca/bookstore or scan the QR code.

Have an upcoming conference or event?
Would you like a gift with valuable content?
Discounts are available on quantity purchases for your organization.
Please email **connect@whenwomentalk.ca** for pricing information.